D1010489

PRESENTED TO

John

FROM

Joel

DATE

12-25-14

ISBN: 978-1-60810-112-2

First Thing Every Morning

Printed and bound in the United States of America.

Published by Simple Truths, LLC
1952 McDowell Road, Suite 300
Naperville, IL 60563
630-946-1460
www.simpletruths.com

Editorial assistance by Todd Hafer
Designed by Thinkpen Design Inc. www.thinkpendesign.com

03-WOZ-12

TURN YOUR LIFE AROUND
ONE DAY AT A TIME

FIRST THING
EVERY
MORNING

LEWIS TIMBERLAKE
WITH ELINOR GRIFFITH

FOREWORD BY DRAYTON MCLANE JR.
CHAIRMAN OF THE MCLANE GROUP AND CEO OF THE HOUSTON ASTROS BASEBALL CLUB

simple truths®
Motivational & Inspirational Gifts

CONTENTS

52 WEEKLY REFLECTIONS AND

365 DAILY QUOTES TO BETTER YOUR LIFE

DEDICATION
A WORD OF THANKS...

As a young man I grew up in a world that was haunted by the lyrics of a song that began, "How do I say thanks for the things you have done for me?"

I find myself now at a similar juncture in my life as I launch this new book. How do I say thanks to so many people who impacted my life, encouraged my life and lifted my life in ways that have allowed me to enjoy a marvelous career over these years...working with the greatest companies and leaders in our free world? Knowing that there is no way for me to recall each name or personally thank each individual for what he or she has done for me, I still wanted to try.

How do I say thanks to people like Drayton McLane and Charles Cawley? Sam Walton and Lee Iacocca? To Paul Harvey and Zig Ziglar? To Alan Brass and Howard E. Butt, Jr.? To Darrell Royal and Tom Landry? To Gordon Peters and Tom Watson, Jr.? The list goes on and on ... Through the years all those who have made my life richer and stronger, who have taught me, who inspired and encouraged me by the lessons they learned as they built great companies or led great movements. People like Dr. Bill Bright, Dr. Adrian Rogers, Dr. Norman Vincent Peale ... and so many others. Individuals whose words encouraged and lives inspired me to try to become more and leave behind a better world, with ideas now captured in *First Thing Every Morning*.

To each of them, and all those I haven't named, but whose influence has been felt and remembered, I offer my undying thanks. It is my hope that somehow, through what I've done in my career and in previous books, I have been able to share how much I have learned from people who "were born to win." People who know that every person can dream great dreams and achieve those dreams. People who truly believe "it's fun to do the impossible." I dedicate this book to you. I promise to continue to do all I can to carry the lamp as you've passed it on to me ... to lift lives and see through a dark and sometimes difficult world, and arrive at a promise that belongs to those who believe "they were born to win."

Finally, I write from a heart full of love to those who have made my life a special joy…

A family that lifts me when I'm low, loves me when I'm unlovable and makes me believe I am the man they think I am.

Friends who "know me and like me anyway," who encourage me by their trust, who accept me by their actions and who keep my feet on firm foundations.

Clients whose beliefs are inspiring, whose concern for their customers is encouraging, whose compassion for their employees is enriching and whose success in the business world is transferable.

A land where all are welcome, everyone is equal and success is a promise, not a platitude.

A God whose presence is personal, whose care is certain, whose promise is dependable and whose love is unexplainable.

Successfully Yours,
Lewis R. Timberlake

PREFACE

LEWIS TIMBERLAKE

What do you do when your whole world crumbles?

Mine took place before I heard of something called the "Gethsemane Principal," which says, "At some time in life, everyone will face their Gethsemane ... when your world crumbles, when everything goes wrong and nothing seems right, and you wonder if anyone knows or cares, when you want to cry instead of 'keepin' on.' You doubt what you believe ... and if you even believe."

My Gethsemane came at a most surprising time in my life.

Up until that moment, it had been a great life. I grew up in Texas and married Georgia Ann, the most beautiful girl in my hometown. I enjoyed a successful career in the life insurance business—even became president of the company. I was president of civic organizations and involved in running campaigns for governors. I'd won awards and honors and ... life was good. My first two children were simply amazing, and my third child, Craig, offered the same promise.

But at age 10, the doctors said he would be blind in two weeks' time. How could that be? Craig had never been sick—never even had a headache.

We discovered there is a gene that can "go bad." It causes Wolfram Syndrome. There is no cure. When it goes bad, bad things happen. First his optic nerve began to die, and I watched my 10-year-old son go blind a little each day. God blessed me with an amazing wife, three phenomenal children and a successful career. But when Craig went blind, my world crumbled. How do you get through that? What do you do?

I cried out in desperation and despair. There was no help available; nobody in high places could sort things out. Then radio broadcaster Paul Harvey told me, "In times like these, it's good remember that there have always been 'times like these.' You can get through this better and stronger, and more able to live life victoriously— *if* you will do some things that help you get through each day."

I realized you must find a way to begin each day in a way that prepares you to say, "Whatever takes place, I shall win. I'll overcome problems and difficulties. I'll look up and not down... I've made up my mind—I believe. I expect God will show us how life turns out best for those who make the best of how life turns out."

That's when I realized I needed to start every day, even challenging and difficult days, with a positive focus. I needed to do the things unsuccessful people won't do. I actually learned, "How you begin the day controls how you go through the day."

Those truths gave me a much-needed handshake of hope.

I credit my high school teacher, Mrs. Crockett, with another life-changing insight. I was born in Stamford, a farm town in West Texas so small that only 3,000 people lived there and that was on a good day. Yet my teacher had an intuitive understanding of human psychology and explained to us, "Whether you think you can or whether you think you can't, you're right"—Henry Ford.

At the time, her message skimmed over my head. But as an adult, when I was stumbling under news of my son's deteriorating health, those words resonated. There is a force, the causality of our actions, that when practiced the first thing every day can change the direction of your or my life. Essentially, we can be immobilized by bad news or take steps to win. The choice is ours.

I'd always dreamed of being a pro baseball player. Mrs. Crockett's words also resonated back then. You see I became a Major League player ... almost. As a kid I wanted to be the world's greatest shortstop. Truth is, baseball was my way to get out of Stamford, Texas. I was drafted into the Army and I played on the baseball team at Fort Ord in California. There were 16 professional baseball players and me, Lewis Timberlake. Del Crandall was catcher, Billy Martin was on second base and I was the shortstop. At nine o'clock on the day we were playing Fort McPherson, Ga., for the Army championship, I agreed to go professional with the St. Louis Cardinals, and even got a bonus check. But at 1:15 p.m., the pitcher, "Vinegar Bend" Mizell, hit me and put me out of the game ... put me out of baseball. Forever!

That's always bugged me. Why? Why is one person physically and physiologically equal to another... and one wins and the other doesn't? Dr. Allan Cox of Harvard studied the top Fortune 500 chief executive officers. The idea was to find a single truth among all the executives that others could adopt to become successful. What did he find? Nine-five percent of the CEOs believed success resulted from their mindset. From Cox's research these three simple truths emerged: 1) Executives are never surprised to win; 2) they never expect to fail and have a goal and plans to overcome obstacles, difficulties and setbacks, and 3) still, they are not afraid to fail; when "knockdowns" occur the executives bounce right back up again. Like Mrs. Crockett said, it's all about how YOU look at things.

So after my baseball setback I bounced back up ... at age 24, into the insurance business. During the first three years of my presidency, the company's sales increased 1,100 percent and grew to be one of the top companies in Texas.

And bounced back again ... at age 37, with my dream to start my own company, Lewis Timberlake & Associates. In seminars, motivational speeches and training programs, I shared what I'd learned and got to know some of America's greatest leaders: Lee Iacocca of Chrysler, Sam Walton of Walmart, Tom Landry of the Dallas Cowboys, Darrell Royal, Zig Ziglar, Paul Harvey, and Dr. Norman Vincent Peale. The "A" list of companies I've helped, some for more than 20 years, starts with American Airlines and the American Heart Association, and includes organizations such as IBM, Publix Supermarkets, Southwestern Bell Telephone, State Farm Insurance Company and National Public Radio.

I have appeared on the same program as Dr. Peter Drucker, the management consultant and author of 39 books, who encouraged me as an individual and made me a better speaker. Others I have shared the stage with include Werner Von Braun, who made a monumental contribution to the space program, and Drayton McLane, one of the greatest business leaders in the country today. Drayton made a monumental success of his company transporting groceries around the world and additionally, took the Houston Astros and made them into a champion baseball team.

Probably the greatest example of Drayton McLane's life is the kind of man he is. He has always been successful, and yet when my youngest son, Craig, died, the next day at 9:00 a.m. Drayton arrived at my house from his home 70 miles away. He walked inside, sat in the living room and said, "I'm here. Whatever you need, whenever you want me, I'm here."

People like that are hard to live up to. But without their example, without their encouragement, without their reassurance that life is worth living, I would not be the man I am today. So I promise that as long as God gives me life, I will continue to try to justify their friendship, share what they've taught me and hopefully make a difference in someone's life!

■

FOREWORD

By Drayton McLane Jr.

CHAIRMAN, McLANE GROUP

CEO, HOUSTON ASTROS

One of the most interesting things to me about the relationship that Lewis Timberlake and I have developed over the years is the way in which we met and how he, one of America's greatest public speakers, always challenges us with such compelling—and worthwhile—ideas. Back then, Lewis was in the insurance business and one of his top agents was Bill Pruett. I got to know Bill through different civic activities here in Temple, Texas, and he told me that he had someone he wanted me to meet and asked if I would have lunch with him if he could work out the arrangements. "Lewis would make a big positive difference," he said. I wholeheartedly agreed. From that lunch on and 40-plus years later, Lewis is still making a real difference.

In about 1973, I asked Lewis if he would meet with our management team at the McLane Company, but it would have to be on a Saturday morning at 7:00. He was not really thrilled with that idea, but he swallowed hard and said he would do it. The company was small then, and our entire leadership group consisted of only about ten people. We met on Saturday mornings once a month for about six months. At that point, it was obvious that Lewis' enthusiasm and mentoring were making a positive difference for the McLane Company and its leadership team. The company grew 30 percent or more every year—from $6 million to $32 billion—for a period of 32 consecutive years and Lewis was a part of that.

We really began to challenge Lewis to the limits when we built divisions in Denver, CO, Tacoma, WA, Athens, GA and Syracuse, NY. He was, at that point, going to each division twice a year. Traveling often, communicating and motivating with a very high level of intensity, Lewis became a mentor to not only ten, but over 250 executives. He now has had an impact on literally thousands of executives and employees at McLane Company, McLane Group and our other related companies. Lewis showed that he was able to grow even faster than we could expand. His uplifting speeches and thought-provoking, fast-paced seminars kept employees focused and helped them seek broader horizons and achieve significant professional and personal goals.

As we have expanded into various other businesses such as plastics manufacturing, food manufacturing, the high technology industry, and Major League Baseball with the Houston Astros, Lewis has been able to adjust and take care of the diverse needs of all of our employees. We know we are not his only client and that many other Fortune 500 companies are on his calendar, but he always makes us feel as if we are the most important one. I have been personally inspired by Lewis, and I have seen him change people's lives for the better and lift them up! The qualities that I value most in Lewis are his integrity, Christian values and his high energy—none of which ever waver.

"When I think of Lewis Timberlake and what he accomplishes, I am always reminded of what Edith Wharton once said, 'There are two ways of spreading the light: to be the candle, or to be the mirror that reflects it.' Lewis is a candle and I enjoy basking in his warmth."

– Drayton McLane Jr.

Some of the best insights from these sessions, the "nuggets" of gold that helped inspire, motivate and transform my leadership team, are now captured in this book, ready for you to benefit!

Lewis Timberlake has a special gift, and I am honored to call him my friend.

DRAYTON MCLANE JR.

CHAIRMAN OF THE MCLANE GROUP AND CEO OF THE HOUSTON ASTROS BASEBALL CLUB
CHAIRMAN, BOARD OF TRUSTEES, SCOTT & WHITE MEMORIAL HOSPITAL
VP OF EXECUTIVE BOARD, BOY SCOUTS OF AMERICA NATIONAL BOARD
BOARD OF TRUSTEES BAYLOR COLLEGE OF MEDICINE

ACKNOWLEDGEMENTS

PRAISE FOR *FIRST THING EVERY MORNING*

"As usual, you are right on target with your new book, *First Thing Every Morning*. I love the approach. I've learned a lot from you, and this book is helpful in a lot of ways."

—REV. PAUL POWELL, FIRST BAPTIST CHURCH, TYLER, TEXAS
RETIRED DEAN, BAYLOR UNIVERSITY THEOLOGICAL SEMINARY

"One of the best in the business wrote it. You are my hero!"

—DELOSS DODDS, ATHLETIC DIRECTOR,
THE UNIVERSITY OF TEXAS AT AUSTIN

"This book has many applications in both personal and professional circumstances. In these frenetic times, *First Thing Every Morning* will serve readers well, allowing a quiet moment for consideration of how best to make the most of each day. This book is worth sharing!"

—ALAN W. BRASS, CEO, PROMEDICA HEALTH SYSTEM

"I have heard nothing but favorable comments about you and your presentation. You must be outstanding, or they wouldn't have you back every year."

—LOU HOLTZ, HEAD FOOTBALL COACH

"Your talk was really great...motivating and entertaining. All of the women's athletic staff was impressed and appreciated the valuable information. Thank you for encouraging all of us to be our best."

—JODY CONRADT, THE UNIVERSITY OF TEXAS

"Your presentation was simply outstanding! I am so inspired and encouraged by what you shared with us, but who you are impressed me even more than what you said."
—RICK EGBERT, DISCOVER FINANCIAL SERVICES

"Our sales force found your remarks both educational and inspirational. Motivating a sales force is a difficult task, and you have helped me to stimulate my people to do the job. I thank you for that."
—JAMES S. LOGDON, VP MARKETING, GTE

"With a combination of humor, emotion, facts and techniques, you wove a web of instructional and motivational thoughts that will be used for a long time to come. Our people have never responded with greater enthusiasm. They were prodded mentally to review themselves, and with such introspection, a growing recognition of things they can do better."
—GLENN BIGGS, FIRST NATIONAL BANK OF SAN ANTONIO

"Your session on Goal Setting was the highlight of the week in our class on Basic Management Development. Ratings were perfect on content and speaker effectiveness. Comments include 'the best pitch I've ever seen in IBM,' 'the best I have ever listened to,' 'fantastic,' 'the most effective speaker I have ever listened to,' and 'I love Lewis.'"
—GEORGE SPENCER, IBM CORP.

INTRODUCTION

HOW THIS BOOK CAN ENERGIZE YOUR LIFE!

I was just thinking about an irrefutable truth: *I can't control what life does to me—but I can control how I react to what life does!*

If that is true—and it is—then that means I must make a choice every day. I can be happy or I can be sad. I can be positive or I can be negative. I can look up or I can look down. It's a choice I can make. It's a choice I must make every single day.

The fact is, we live in a very negative world. Radio commentator Paul Harvey once told me that 93.7 percent of what you and I see and hear each day is "bad news." For example, instead of "80 percent chance of sun," we have "20 percent chance of rain!" If you really want a good day every day, it's up to you to do the things successful people do. This book is filled with these things.

One of the *best* ways to have a good day is to start the day right. *First Thing Every Morning* is designed to help you do just that ... by beginning each day with a short reflection that lifts your spirits and lightens your load. It will set the tone for the rest of the day. And when you start the day reading this book, you will soon see it's not the outlook, but the uplook, that matters. Far too many people tell me, "I'll believe it when I see it!" No-no-no...you'll see it when you believe it!

One of the people who made a positive impact on America—and the world—is Dr. Will James, a pioneering American psychologist and philosopher. One of his best-known gifts was this discovery in the 1880s, something that's equally true today: "Human beings, by changing the inner attitudes of their minds, can change the outer aspects of their lives."

With the phrase ringing in my head ("The only thing to do with good advice is pass it on."), I have ideas to share about the book. From its title, *First Thing Every*

Morning, you already know the ideal time ... right when you get up. Get out of bed on the *first* ring of the alarm. Now don't laugh, but the repetitive action, difficult at first, will turn into a good habit. I've read many reports from those who study "Sleep Learning." They say the first 18-37 minutes of the day determine the way you will go through the day. You can work through the book sequentially, one section for each week with a supporting quote-a-day. Ten to fifteen minutes a day. Don't rush. This distillation is from some of the best minds in the world, stretching back in time. Your reflections on the material for the "What Do You Think?" part can be life-changing or certainly life-affirming! Or check the Table of Contents for topics that relate to your situation and skip from section to section.

Born to Win

Energize your life with these self-help books by Lewis Timberlake: *Born to Win* and *It's Always Too Soon to Quit*. Over 100,000 people have bought the best-selling *Born to Win* and helped turn their dreams into reality. And as Zig Ziglar says about *It's Always Too Soon to Quit*, this book "inspires us to reach higher rungs on the ladder." Both books are available at: www.lewistimberlake.com.

During the day surround yourself with **P**ositive **R**einforcers—think of it as good **PR**. Among my favorite PR activities:

Sing in the shower, while you dress, in the car, when you're mowing the grass. ...We don't sing because we're happy; we're happy because we sing!

Turn off or delay watching the morning news (often a downer!).

Plan your goals for the day.

Around the breakfast table, make it a habit of "seating" the day right. In our family, each person must share one good thing that happened the day before and one good thing we expect to happen today.

Listen to motivational content as you exercise or drive in the car. A study at UCLA on the average amount of time people spend in the car reveals: You could have the equivalent of three years of college in only six years! So use it positively.

As you stockpile the positive news, here's another tip: Write down favorite quotes from the book. Put them in your wallet or up on a bathroom mirror.

Copy them into your iPhone or e-mail them to friends. This reinforces the ideas and makes them belong to Y-O-U. One of my favorite quotes came from John Wooden. My daughter decoupaged a copy, and now it occupies a prominent place on my desk: "Things always turn out best for those who make the best of how life turns out." Dr. John McKitter of the University of Texas often talked about an "engram." That's the notion that after you hear or read something six times, it changes your neurological tissue and forms a memory. So surround yourself with positive sayings and ideas, AND keep repeating them.

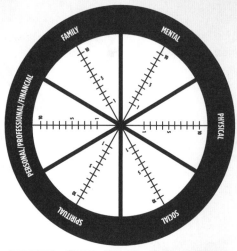

THE CIRCLE OF LIFE

Instructions: Rate yourself in every area of life. Plot the numbers in the corresponding sections on the circle above. (one being low to ten being high). Complete your map by connecting the dots. This map gives a picture of where you currently are. You will use this to see how far you have to go to achieve a "Balanced Life."

Finally, since the purpose of *First Thing Every Morning* is to help you create a more balanced, happier and more successful life, there's a big question that remains: *How can I apply the book's reflections to ALL aspects of my life ... with real effectiveness?* Each of us has a "Circle of Life" with six components that compete for our precious time: Business, Financial, Family, Social, Physical, Spiritual, and Mental.

Ideally, each of these areas has written goals (short, intermediate and long-range ones). The six areas make up our "full-life" and our potential. You can contact my office at Lewis Timberlake & Associates, P.O. Box 26745, Austin,

Texas, 78755, if you want to see the materials that are available to help you look at your life and develop goals for all the areas of your life.

Welcome to a better day ... a better life ... and a better Y-O-U! Today is the first day of the rest of your life. And it begins when you read *First Thing Every Morning*!

"Faith is the bird that sings when the dawn is still dark."

–RABINDRANATH TAGORE
INDIAN POET AND NOBEL PRIZE LAUREATE

I WAS JUST THINKING ABOUT ... FAITH

I get a lot of letters. Folks are always sending me letters with quotes, stories and jokes. I look forward to getting them, and I enjoy them all very much. However, sometimes I'll get one that is extremely eye-opening. For example, I just received the following e-mail on faith from a special friend:

God is like General Electric—He lights your path.

God is like Bayer Aspirin—He works wonders.

God is like Hallmark Cards—He cares enough to send the very best.

God is like Allstate—You're in good hands.

God is like Tide detergent—He gets out the stains others leave behind.

God is like Alka-Seltzer—Oh, what a relief He is.

God is like Scotch Tape—You can't see Him, but you know He is there.

God is like Duracell batteries—nothing outlasts Him.

God is like American Express—never leave home without Him.

God is like Delta—He is ready when you are.

Here is the point I am trying to make—don't be afraid to belong to God!

WHAT DO YOU THINK?

_____

_____

_____

_____

6 MORE THOUGHTS FOR YOUR WEEK: FAITH

"Faith is taking the first step even when you don't see the whole staircase."

MARTIN LUTHER KING JR.

"The Lord stands above the new day, for God has made it. All restlessness, all impurity, all worry and anxiety flee before him."

DIETRICH BONHOEFFER

"Faith, like a jackal, feeds among the tombs, and even from these dead doubts she gathers her most vital hope."

HERMAN MELVILLE

"To one who has faith, no explanation is necessary. To one without faith, no explanation is possible."

ST. THOMAS AQUINAS

An atheist complained to a friend because Christians have their special holidays such as Christmas and Easter, and Jews celebrate their national holidays such as Passover and Yom Kippur. "But we atheists," he said, "have no recognized national holiday. It is unfair discrimination." To which his friend replied, "Why don't you celebrate April 1st?"

FROM THE SPEAKER'S QUOTE BOOK BY ROY B. ZUCK

"I know God will never give me anything I can't handle. I just wish He didn't trust me so much."

MOTHER TERESA

"The two most powerful warriors are patience and time."

LEO TOLSTOY

I WAS JUST THINKING ABOUT ... GOALS

Dr. Viktor Frankl spent years in a concentration camp during World War II. He says that the prisoner who lost faith in the future—faith in his aims and goals for his life—was doomed. "With the loss of belief in the future," said Frankl, an Austrian psychiatrist and author of *Man's Search for Meaning*, "he also lost his spiritual hold. He let himself decline and become subject to mental and physical decay."

Without a meaningful, significant goal, life becomes a deadly, dull existence. During times of testing, our will to fight is lessened, and we often just give up and quit. It's true for animals, too. I once read a story by U.S. Senate Chaplain Frederick Brown Harris about a group of whales that, while pursuing sardines, found themselves marooned in a small bay—a bay that proved to be a death trap for the large animals. Rev. Harris explained, "The fish lured the sea giants to their deaths. They came to their violent demise by chasing small ends, by prostituting vast powers for insignificant goals."

Consider this story: In 1922, a 38-year-old man who went bankrupt in the clothing business went home and told his wife, "I can't die like this. I know I was born to do something more." She said, "I believe in you," and together they wrote a goal for his life.

Twenty-three years later, in 1945, that same man was president of the United States of America. ... His name? Harry S. Truman. His favorite verse of scripture was Jeremiah 29:11, which he would read every morning. "For I know the plans I have for you," says the Lord. "They are plans for your good, not for disaster, to give you a future and a hope."

WHAT DO YOU THINK?

_____

_____

_____

6 MORE THOUGHTS FOR YOUR WEEK: GOALS

"Don't bunt. Aim out of the ballpark.
Aim for the company of immortals."
DAVID OGILVY

"Where there is no vision, the people perish."
PROVERBS 29:18

"We succeed only as we identify in life, or in war, or in
anything else, a single overriding objective, and make
all other considerations bend to that one objective."
PRESIDENT DWIGHT D. EISENHOWER

"Obstacles are those frightful things you
see when you take your eyes off your goal."
HENRY FORD

"It is possible that the man who doesn't
know his own mind hasn't missed a thing."
LESTER D. KLIMEK

"Never measure the height of a mountain until you
have reached the top. Then you will see how low it was."
DAG HAMMARSKJOLD

■

"The greatest discovery of my generation is that a human being can alter his life by altering his attitudes of mind."

WILLIAM JAMES

PSYCHOLOGIST AND PHILOSOPHER

I WAS JUST THINKING ABOUT ... ATTITUDE

Our problem is NOT our problem. Our problem is our ATTITUDE about our problem!

In 15th century Europe, the whole continent was filled with despair. It was probably the most discouraging time in European history. In 1492, a German newspaper, *The Nuremburg Chronicle,* had an article stating that the end had come; there was nothing left worth living for. At the close of this article was a blank page on which the reader could fill in any discouraging events or situations that had been left out. The next year, Christopher Columbus came home saying, "There's a whole new world out there! Quit looking down and start looking up!" There were still problems, but now people looked at them with a different attitude!

Maybe that idea is why J. Sidlow Baxter wrote, "What is the difference between an obstacle and an opportunity? Our attitude toward it. Every opportunity has a difficulty and every difficulty has an opportunity." Just think about what was accomplished when these people were imprisoned:

- *Robinson Crusoe* was written when Daniel Defoe was in prison.
- John Bunyan wrote his best-selling book *The Pilgrim's Progress* in the Bedford Jail.
- Sir Walter Raleigh compiled *The History of the World* during a 13-year imprisonment.
- Martin Luther translated the Bible while confined in the castle of Wartburg.
- Nelson Mandela, during his 27 years in prison, started work secretly on his autobiography, *Long Walk to Freedom*. He went on to become president of South Africa.

In other words, our problem is NOT our problem. Our problem is our ATTITUDE about our problem!

I heard this story from Ronald Reagan when he was governor of California. He was speaking to a convention of businesspeople to encourage them. His theme was attitude, not aptitude, controls altitude. "Along with a positive attitude, we must have a positive plan," the governor said.

In case there's any doubt remaining about attitude, Nobel Laureate George Bernard Shaw can have the last word. Who can forget the classic movie *My Fair Lady*, based on his play *Pygmalion,* and how Audrey Hepburn is transformed from a poor Cockney flower girl into a sophisticated aristocrat? Shaw said, "I can't control what life did to me, but I can control how I react. Therein lies the difference."

WHAT DO YOU THINK?

_____
_____
_____
_____
_____
_____
_____
_____
_____
_____
_____
_____
_____
_____
_____
_____
_____
_____
_____
_____
_____
_____

6 MORE THOUGHTS FOR YOUR WEEK:
POSITIVE ATTITUDE

"Optimism is the faith that leads to achievement.
Nothing can be done without hope and confidence."

HELEN KELLER

"The positive thinker sees the invisible, feels the
intangible and achieves the impossible."

ROBERT SCHULLER

"Two men look out through the same bars;
one sees mud, the other sees stars."

REV. FREDERICK LANGBRIDGE

"Hardening of the attitudes is the most
deadly disease on the face of the earth."

ZIG ZIGLAR

"A pessimist sees the difficulty in every opportunity;
an optimist sees the opportunity in every difficulty."

WINSTON CHURCHILL

"Optimism supplies the basic energy of civilization. Optimism doesn't
wait on facts. It deals with prospects. Pessimism is a waste of time."

NORMAN COUSINS

■

"Success is going from failure to failure without losing your enthusiasm."

WINSTON CHURCHILL

I WAS JUST THINKING ABOUT …

OVERCOMING FAILURE

I got to meet Tom Watson Jr.—the son of the founder of IBM. We had breakfast at the IBM Educational Center in New York. I enjoyed every minute, but one thing he said has permeated my thoughts even to this day, "The only time you can't afford to fail is the last time you try."

That helps me better understand a "lifetime failure." The man had gone from one failure to another, one debt to another. His left hand was useless because of a war injury. He had held several government jobs and failed at all of them. He had even served time in prison! Finally, he picked up a pen and wrote a book that has thrilled the world for centuries. The failure: Cervantes. The success: *Don Quixote*.

Or think about the greatest of all American poets, who was a failure for some 20 years! He was 39 before he ever sold a volume of poetry. Yet today he is considered one of the finest writers ever. His poems have been published in some 22 languages, and he won the Pulitzer Prize for poetry four times! He had more honorary degrees bestowed upon him than probably any other man of letters and Congress named him an American Poet Laureate—Robert Frost!

Robert Frost learned a valuable lesson: We may fail, but we are not failures! Lots of people have their hopes dashed and dreams shattered. But when achievers fail, they see failure as only temporary, and they decide to rise above adversity by turning tribulations into triumphs, failures into fortunes and burdens into blessings. Remember, failure is the backdoor to success.

Taking Their Hits!
- **Cy Young** is supposedly the best pitcher of all time. He won 511 victories, but he lost **315 games**.
- Swimmer **Mark Spitz** thought he had failed. He promised five gold medals at the Olympics in Mexico City. He won **only two** then, but four years later he won seven.
- **Babe Ruth** struck out 1,330 times—but he hit 714 home runs!

WHAT DO YOU THINK?

A Keepsake: I've kept this inspirational quote in my wallet for years. By an unknown author, the words give a new perspective on "failure" and have helped me through many tough times of testing.

• Failing doesn't mean I'm a failure; it just means I haven't yet succeeded.

• Failing doesn't mean I've accomplished nothing; it just means I've learned something.

• Failing doesn't mean I've been a fool; it just means I had enough faith to experiment.

• Failing doesn't mean I've been disgraced; it just means I dared to try.

• Failing doesn't mean I don't have what it takes; it just means I must do things differently next time.

• Failing doesn't mean I'm inferior; it just means I'm not perfect.

• Failing doesn't mean I've wasted my time; it just means I have a reason to start over.

• Failing doesn't mean I should give up; it just means I must try harder.

• Failing doesn't mean I'll never make it; it just means I'll need more patience.

• Failing doesn't mean I'm wrong; it just means I must find a better way.

• Failing doesn't mean God has abandoned me; it just means I must obediently seek His will.

6 MORE THOUGHTS FOR YOUR WEEK:
OVERCOMING FAILURE

"History has demonstrated that the most notable winners usually encountered heartbreaking obstacles before they triumphed. They finally won because they refused to become discouraged by their defeats. Disappointments acted as a challenge. Don't let difficulties discourage you."

B.C. FORBES, THE FOUNDER OF *Forbes*

"Mountaintops are for views and inspiration, but fruit is grown in the valleys."

BILLY GRAHAM

"The real legacy of my life was my biggest failure.
Being sent to prison was the beginning of God's greatest use of my life!"

CHUCK COLSON

"The man of character finds a special attractiveness in difficulty, since it is only by coming to grips with difficulty that he can realize his potentialities."

PRESIDENT CHARLES DE GAULLE

"Don't be discouraged by failure. Failure, in a sense, is the highway to success because every discovery of what is false leads us to seek what is true. And every fresh experience points out an error which we shall, afterwards, carefully avoid."

JOHN KEATS

"Failure is never final and success is never ending. Success is a journey, not a destination."

ROBERT SCHULLER

"Hope is the power of being cheerful in circumstances which we know to be desperate."

G.K. CHESTERTON

I WAS JUST THINKING ABOUT …
LIFE'S TOUGHEST CHALLENGES

Everyone at sometime in life faces his or her own Gethsemane. This is the time when the heart hurts through the night, and you wonder whether or not you still love life, even whether or not you still love God. But don't give up, because I've got good news for you.

Consider this story. A young man was standing on the snow-covered shores of Lake Michigan one wintry night, ready to jump. He was a 32-year-old bankrupt dropout. As he was standing there, a chilling thought flashed through his mind, *Do I have the right to end my life?* The answer was clear—clear as the majesty of that moonlight. You have no right to eliminate yourself. You are responsible for grabbing hold of life.

The young man turned his back on the deathly waters and instead set himself out on a remarkable career. "Bucky," as his friends called him, made a choice that later changed the lives of many people. Best known as the inventor of the geodesic dome, he held more than 170 patents at the time of his death, and he was world famous as an engineer, mathematician, architect, philosopher and poet. His name: R. Buckminster Fuller.

The point of his life seems to be proving that more men fail through lack of purpose than through lack of talent. Mary Wilcox wrote, "The world is round, and the place itself that seems like the end may only be the beginning." The proof of this lies in history itself:

Wilma Rudolph, the 20th of 22 children, overcame crippling childhood polio to win three gold medals in the 1960 Olympics. Called the "Tornado," she became "the fastest woman on earth."

Thomas Edison's teacher told his mother her son was "too dumb to learn."

The parents of Albert Einstein thought he was mentally inferior because he never spoke until he was three years old.

Walt Disney started his career with $40 cash in his pocket and debts totaling $200. In fact, he was bankrupt years later when he took his *Steamboat Willie* idea to Hollywood.

John Milton was blind when he wrote his most sublime poetry, *Paradise Lost.*

Richard Byrd, an outstanding pilot who was the first to reach the South Pole, crash-landed the first two times he soloed. The third time he flew alone and flew head-on into another plane ... but he hung on.

Theodor Geisel suffered over 28 rejections before he sold his first children's book ... and became Dr. Seuss. His books have now sold over 200 million copies in 50 different languages!

In the French and Indian War, at Fort Necessity, a young American officer surrendered to the enemy—but we forget about that because George Washington later became president of the United States.

In other words, people can get deeply discouraged. But filled with God's power and fueled by God's presence, you can hang in, hold on—and win! These people are not exceptions. They're just people who refused to be held down by daunting circumstances and deep despair.

Think about how a grain of sand gets inside the oyster's shell and wounds the oyster. A liquid is secreted that begins to coat that grain of sand in order to protect the oyster from further damage. With time and pressure, a priceless pearl (and relief from pain) is created. The oyster accomplishes nothing worthwhile unless it is hurt first. Just as steel gains its strength only after being sent through the fiery furnace, and just as coal turns into diamonds only after centuries of pressure and friction, so people (like YOU!) can and do become stronger through the tests and trials of life.

How do you react to the most difficult circumstances of your life? Do you give up and moan, or do you get up and move?

6 MORE THOUGHTS FOR YOUR WEEK:
LIFE'S TOUGHEST CHALLENGES

"All things are difficult before they are easy."

–JOHN NORLEY

"Fight one more round. When your feet are so tired that you have to shuffle back to the center of the ring, fight one more round! When you are so tired that you want to give up, fight one more round! When you feel beaten and conquered by life's storms, fight one more round. When you are exhausted, tired, weary and worn, fight one more round!"

–JAMES CORBETT

"Consider every mistake you do make as an asset."

–PAUL J. MEYER

"The marvelous richness of the human experience would lose something of its rewarding joy if there were not limitations to overcome. The hilltop would not be half so wonderful if there were not dark valleys to traverse."

–HELEN KELLER

"Crises force our attention on the disorder in our thinking and can save us as we teeter on the brink of an even greater disaster."

–DAVID MCNALLY

"The truth is that our finest moments are most likely to occur when we are feeling deeply uncomfortable, unhappy, or unfulfilled. For it is only in such moments, propelled by our discomfort, that we are likely to step out of our ruts and start searching for different ways or truer answers."

–M. SCOTT PECK

■

"Concern yourself
not with what you
tried and failed in,
but with what is
still possible
for you to do."

–POPE JOHN XXIII
264TH CATHOLIC POPE

I WAS JUST THINKING ABOUT ... A FRESH START

A report from UCLA said, "Every great person who ever lived first faced total, complete, abject failure." Let me remind you how important it is to close the door on failings and start again.

Once when I was in New York, Dr. Norman Vincent Peale, the brilliant author of *The Power of Positive Thinking* which has sold seven million copies, told me a story I can never forget. Dr. Peale did some research on a man who came through a difficult childhood to have this happen:

Less than one year of formal schooling
Failed in business in 1831
Defeated for the legislature in 1832
Again failed in business in 1833
Fiancée died in 1835
Suffered a nervous breakdown in 1836
Defeated for Speaker in 1838
Defeated for Elector in 1840
Married in 1842, but wife was burden
Only one of his four sons lived beyond age 18
Defeated for Congress in 1843
Defeated for Congress in 1848
Defeated for Senate in 1855
Defeated for Vice President in 1856
Defeated for Senate in 1858
Elected President in 1860

Begin Again, Begin!
Life can be an uphill climb that
is full of hidden pain.
The sun, it seems, is never out.
Dark skies and dreary only.

A broken heart, some shattered dreams,
are scattered all around.
Your highest hopes like feathers blown
come fluttering to the ground.

It seems the weight of all the world
has crushed the spirit within.
But suddenly you hear a voice,
Begin again, begin.

You have the strength to start anew;
it's hidden deep inside.
The courage that you beckon forth
is constant as the tide.

The failures that you've had before,
will never come again.
It's time to start your life anew,
Begin again, begin.

– UNKNOWN POET

Who was that man? Abraham Lincoln, who many consider our greatest president.

There's an idea I want to share that can revitalize your thoughts. "Well Managed Failure" is a term coined by William Marsten who wrote, "Every success I know has been reached because the person was able to analyze defeat and actually profit by it in the next undertaking." Well-managed failure is one of opportunity's favorite disguises, waiting for a fresh start.

One of the greatest examples of this concept happened a century ago. George Washington Carver said, "Ninety-nine percent of the failures come from people who have the habit of making excuses." In 1915, Carver and the other residents of Coffee City, AL, had every reason to make excuses—they were nearly starving due to the destruction of the cotton crop by boll weevils. But rather than make excuses for the situation, Carver suggested growing peanuts instead of cotton. Day after day he then developed innovative uses for peanuts, making soaps, plastics, inks, chemicals and cosmetics from peanut-derived substances. Little Coffee City prospered from this no-nonsense, no-excuse handling of the cotton crop disaster.

And, while thinking of fresh starts, Dara Torres swims into mind. At age 41, Dara came out of retirement to earn a spot on the 2008 U.S. Olympic swim team--setting an American record in the 50-meter freestyle at the Olympic Trials. She went on to win three silver medals at the Beijing Games. This marked the third time Torres had come out of retirement, and she has announced her intention to compete in the 2012 Olympics, at age 45.

There is a secret that you and I must believe if we are going to achieve our dreams … *each day brings a fresh start!*

WHAT DO YOU THINK?

---

6 MORE THOUGHTS FOR YOUR WEEK:
A FRESH START

"Failure is the opportunity to begin again ... more intelligently."
—HENRY FORD

"We are not animals. We are not a product of what has
happened to us in our past. We have the power of choice."
—STEPHEN COVEY

"Each indecision brings its own delays and days are lost lamenting
over lost days. ... What you can do or think you can do, begin it.
For boldness has magic, power and genius in it."
— JOHANN WOLFGANG VON GOETHE

"Supposing you have tried and failed again and again. You may have
a fresh start any moment you choose, for this thing that we call
'failure' is not the falling down, but the staying down."
—MARY PICKFORD

"Choose always the way that seems the best, however rough it may be.
Custom will soon render it easy and agreeable."
—PYTHAGORAS

"Renew thyself completely each day; do it again, and again, and forever again."
—CHINESE INSCRIPTION

"The highest reward for a person's toil is not what they get for it, but what they become by it."

—JOHN RUSKIN
BRITISH SCHOLAR

I WAS JUST THINKING ABOUT …
THE FINISH LINE

We are judged, not by what we start, but by what we finish. One worthwhile task carried to a successful conclusion is worthy of 50 half-finished tasks.

A plaque in the Kipling Room of the Toronto Library reads, "What you do when you don't have to determines exactly what you will be when you can no longer help it."

Consider this person's run to his life's finish line. George had fallen to the depth of despair by poverty and bankruptcy, and was forced to retire from public life a defeated man. He wandered darkened London streets convinced he was without a friend anywhere in the world. A cerebral hemorrhage paralyzed his right side. He could hardly walk. He could not move his right hand. The doctors gave him no hope of recovering.

Day-to-Day Truths

Someone sent me a wonderful "wish" that I now pass on. As you contemplate the finish line, may you have:

- Enough successes to keep you eager
- Enough failure to keep you humble
- Enough joy to share with others
- Enough trials to keep you strong
- Enough hope to keep you happy
- Enough faith to banish depression
- Enough determination to make each day better than yesterday

And then one night while in total despair, facing debtors prison again, he met an amateur poet named Charles Jennens. Charles had a manuscript and asked George to compose a score for it. In a matter of days, working feverishly and rarely leaving his room, George Friedrich Handel composed an oratorio. It was first performed in Dublin in 1742 and today is one of the most famous religious oratorios of all time—the *Messiah*.

It really comes down to a simple truth, captured in this simple story…

A loving mother once gave her small son a nickel to buy some candy. He went from place to place and studied each assortment with the utmost care. His mother, tired of waiting, called to him, "Hurry up, son! Spend your money—we have to get going."

"But Mama," he replied, "I've only got one nickel, so I have to spend it carefully."

You only have one life to spend, so spend it very carefully.

WHAT DO YOU THINK?

_____

_____

_____

_____

_____

_____

_____

_____

_____

_____

_____

_____

_____

_____

_____

_____

_____

_____

_____

6 MORE THOUGHTS FOR YOUR WEEK:
THE FINISH LINE

"It is decidedly not true that 'nice guys finish last,' as that highly original American baseball philosopher, Leo Durocher, was alleged to have said."

–ALAN GREENSPAN

"If you want to be remembered after you're dead, write something worth reading or do something worth writing about."

–BENJAMIN FRANKLIN

"To finish strong, you first have to begin."

–DAN GREEN

"Watch your thoughts; they become words.
Watch your words; they become actions.
Watch your actions; they become habits.
Watch your habits; they become character.
Watch your character; it becomes *your* destiny".

–FRANK OUTLAW

"Every man must decide whether he will walk in the light of creative altruism or in the darkness of destructive selfishness."

–MARTIN LUTHER KING JR.

"Be ashamed to die until you have won some victory for humanity."

–HORACE MANN

"There is a way to do it better. Find it."

—THOMAS EDISON

INVENTOR AND SCIENTIST

CHANGING YOUR LIFE –TODAY!

How difficult life can be. People are tossed and turned by all the demands of too much to do and never enough time to do it. Bills pile up and money just won't stretch. That's why I appreciate the following suggestions sent to me by someone who understood—and cared—and wanted me to "come apart before I come apart!"

JUST FOR TODAY I will try to live through this day only and not tackle all my problems at once. I can do something for twelve hours that would appall me if I felt that I had to keep it up for a lifetime.

JUST FOR TODAY I will be happy. This assumes that what Abraham Lincoln said is true: "Most folks are as happy as they make up their minds to be."

JUST FOR TODAY I will adjust myself to what is, and I will not try to adjust everything to my own desires. I will take my "luck" as it comes and fit myself to it.

JUST FOR TODAY I will exercise my soul in three ways: I will do somebody a good turn and not get found out—if anybody knows it, it will not count. I will do at least two things that I don't want to do—just for exercise. I will not show anyone that my feelings are hurt—they may hurt, but today, I will not show it.

JUST FOR TODAY I will have a quiet half hour all by myself. During this half hour, I will read God's Word … and I will spend time praying and listening to Him.

JUST FOR TODAY I will be unafraid. Especially, I will not be afraid to enjoy what is beautiful and to believe that as I give to the world, the world gives to me.

JUST FOR TODAY I will remember the promise of Philippians 4:13—"I can do all things, through Christ, who strengthens me."

WHAT DO YOU THINK?

6 MORE THOUGHTS FOR YOUR WEEK: CHANGE

"Light tomorrow with today."

–ELIZABETH BARRETT BROWNING

"No man need live a minute longer as he is because the
Creator endowed him with the ability to change himself."

–J.C. PENNEY

"Never doubt that a small group of thoughtful, committed citizens
can change the world. Indeed, it is the only thing that ever has."

–MARGARET MEAD

"What can you do to promote world peace? Go home and love your family."

–MOTHER TERESA

"See everything. Overlook a great deal. Improve a little."

–POPE JOHN XXIII

"If you don't like something, change it.
If you can't change it, change your attitude."

–MAYA ANGELOU

"Don't pray when it rains if you don't pray when the sun shines."

— SATCHEL PAIGE

BASEBALL PLAYER

I WAS JUST THINKING ABOUT …
THE POWER OF PRAYER

Prayer was the secret of Jesus' life. Every moment of His life was bathed in prayer. The one thing the apostles asked Jesus was "teach us to pray." Satan trembles when he sees a Christian on his knees! I once heard a great preacher teach seven steps to effective praying (Matthew 6:9):

First: Approach God with confidence and reverence …
Our Father, who art in heaven,
Hallowed be Thy name.

Second: Be concerned about His concern …
Thy kingdom come.

Third: Commit yourself to obey Him …
Thy will be done
On earth as it is in heaven.

Fourth: Depend on God to provide your needs …
Give us this day our daily bread.

Fifth: Empty your heart of guilt and grudges …
And forgive us our trespasses,
As we forgive those who trespass against us.

Sixth: Fortify yourself against temptation...
And lead us not into temptation,
But deliver us from evil.

Seventh: Glorify God for answered prayers...
For Thine is the kingdom and power and glory forever!

Pray ... Pray the first thing in the morning, the last thing at night and in-between. Your thanks will be heard, your heartaches eased and, in the way God knows best, your prayers answered.

WHAT DO YOU THINK?

_____

_____

_____

_____

_____

_____

_____

_____

_____

_____

_____

_____

_____

_____

6 MORE THOUGHTS FOR YOUR WEEK: PRAYER

"Grow flowers of gratitude in the soil of prayer."
—VERBENA WOODS

"'Have faith in God,' Jesus answered. 'Therefore I tell you, whatever you ask for in prayer, believe that you will receive it, and it will be yours.'"
—MARK 11:22-24

"Prayer is when you talk to God; meditation is when you listen to God."
—DIANA ROBINSON

"Thank God every morning when you get up that you have something to do that day which must be done, whether you like it or not. Being forced to work, and forced to do your best, will breed in you temperance and self-control, diligence and strength of will, cheerfulness and contentment, and a hundred virtues which the idle will never know."
—CHARLES KINGSLEY

"There came a time in my life when I earnestly prayed, 'God, I want Your power!' Time wore on and the power did not come. One day the burden was more than I could bear. 'God, why haven't You answered the prayer?' God seemed to whisper back His simple reply, 'With plans no bigger than yours, you don't need My power.'"
—CARL BATES

"Many people pray as if God were a big aspirin pill;
they come only when they hurt."
—B. GRAHAM DIENERT

■

"Make the most
of yourself,
for that is all
there is of you."

–RALPH WALDO EMERSON

ESSAYIST, PHILOSOPHER AND POET

I WAS JUST THINKING ABOUT ... RULES FOR LIFE

Over the years, a great many people have cared enough about me to share "seeds of thought" that have made a big difference in my life. I decided to combine my favorites into a list.

I've learned that:

- The harder you work, the luckier you get.
- You can do something in an instant that will give you heartache for life.
- You can "keep on keeping on" long after you think you can't.
- Either you control your attitude or it controls you.
- Money is a lousy way of keeping score.
- If you treat a person like the person you want them to be, they will do their best to become that person.
- My best friend and I can do anything or nothing and have the best time.
- True friendship continues to grow–even over the longest distance.
- Just because someone doesn't love you the way you want them to doesn't mean they don't love you with all they have.
- No matter how badly your heart is broken, the world doesn't stop for your grief.
- Our background and circumstances may have influenced who we are, but we are ultimately responsible for what we become.
- Credentials on the wall do not make you a decent human being.

Words to Live By
- The six most important words:
I admit I made a mistake.
- The five most important words:
You did a good job.
- The four most important words:
What is YOUR opinion?
- The three most important words:
If you please.
- The two most important words:
Thank you.
- The one most important word: We.
- The least important word: I.
–Author Unknown

- The people you care about most in life are taken from you too soon.
- God is the source of love.
- Making a living is not the same as making a life.
- Even when I have pains, I don't have to be one.
- I still have a lot to learn.

And while pondering these "Rules of Life," remember Admiral Hyman Rickover's observations about people, "Great minds discuss ideas, average minds discuss events, small minds discuss people." Always strive to be G-R-E-A-T, even in little things you do.

WHAT DO YOU THINK?

Are You a Samaritan?
"I shall not pass this way again; let me now relieve some pain, remove some barrier from the road, or lighten someone's heavy load."
–Eva Rose York

6 MORE THOUGHTS FOR YOUR WEEK:
RULES FOR LIFE

"You either have to be first, best or different."

–LORETTA LYNN

"All of the animals, excepting man,
know that the principal business of life is to enjoy it."

–SAMUEL BUTLER

"The greatest danger for most of us is not that our aim is too high
and we miss it, but that it is too low and we reach it."

–MICHELANGELO

"Too often we underestimate the power of a touch, a smile,
a kind word, a listening ear, an honest compliment, or the smallest
act of caring, all of which have the potential to turn a life around."

–LEO BUSCAGLIA

"An apology is the superglue of life. It can repair just about anything."

–LYNN JOHNSTON

"To eat, to love, to sing, and to digest; in truth,
these are the four acts of the comic opera known as life,
and they pass like bubbles in a bottle of champagne."

–GIOACCHINO ROSSINI

"God sweetens outward pain with inward peace."

–THOMAS WATSON
ENGLISH CLERGYMAN

I WAS JUST THINKING ABOUT … GOD

Everywhere I travel, I see signs and billboards that some person used to send a special message to America. The more I think about them, the more powerful their meaning becomes:

- Let's meet at my house on Sunday before the game! –God
- C'mon over, and bring the kids! –God
- What part of "Thou Shalt Not" do you not understand? –God
- We need to talk! –God
- That "Love Thy Neighbor" thing … I mean it! –God
- You think it is hot here? –God
- Have you read my No. 1 bestseller? There will be a test! –God

I think the people posting these signs realize that everyone occupies some kind of pulpit and preaches some sort of sermon every day!

I also see constant signs around me of how God uses broken things. He takes broken soil to produce a crop, broken clouds to give rain, broken grain to give bread, broken bread to give strength. … It is the broken alabaster box that gives forth perfume. It is Peter, weeping bitterly, who returns to greater power than ever.

You could say David W. Hartman was broken. After all, he went blind when he was 8 years old. But he still held on to his dream, even when that dream was shattered by Temple University Medical School telling him that nobody without eyesight had ever completed medical school. He courageously faced the challenge of "reading" medical books by having 25 complete textbooks audio-recorded for him. And guess what? At 27, David W. Hartman became the first blind student to complete medical school in the United States.

"Each of us is disabled in one way or another," Dr. Hartman, now a psychiatrist, told 597 graduates at Gettysburg College. "Some of us are shy, some of us are over-confident ... the important thing is how we deal with those disabilities."

You might say, "Great minds have dreams, all others only have wishes!" and behind the scenes, helping us to realize our potential, is God.

WHAT DO YOU THINK?

_____

_____

_____

_____

_____

_____

_____

_____

_____

_____

_____

_____

_____

_____

_____

_____

_____

_____

6 MORE THOUGHTS FOR YOUR WEEK: GOD

"God loves each of us as if there were only one of us."

–St. Augustine

"The soul can split the sky in two and let the face of God shine through."

–Edna St. Vincent Millay

"Have courage for the great sorrows of life and patience
for the small ones. And when you have finished your daily task,
go to sleep in peace. God is awake."

–Victor Hugo

"God does not die on the day when we cease to believe
in a personal deity, but we die on the day when our lives cease
to be illuminated by the steady radiance, renewed daily,
of a wonder, the source of which is beyond all reason."

–Dag Hammarskjold

"I could prove God statistically."

– George Gallup

"Your mind cannot possibly understand God. Your heart already knows.
Minds were designed for carrying out the orders of the heart."

–Emmanuel

■

"The best way
to prepare
for life is to
begin to live."

–ELBERT HUBBARD
AMERICAN WRITER AND PHILOSOPHER

I WAS JUST THINKING ABOUT ... PERSPECTIVE

As I listen to the news and hear person after person talking about how difficult it is to have hope in "times like these," I remember a letter I got from a friend who is 91 years young and puts world happenings in perspective. Here's what he said:

"America's elders lived through the great 1929 stock market crash that was called the Depression Years, Pearl Harbor, the loss of the Philippines, years of long days and nights in defense plants in the 1940s, fighting in Europe and the Pacific, D-Day, the Battle of the Bulge, V-E Day, the hope-filled beginning of the United Nations in America, the A-bomb, the Marshall Plan in Europe, the Berlin airlift, war in Korea, the U-2 incident, the Bay of Pigs invasion, the Cuban missile crisis, the killing of President Kennedy, the killing of Bobby Kennedy, the killing of Martin Luther King Jr., the civil rights struggle, the Vietnam War, Americans on the moon, Watergate and the subsequent resignation of a president and vice president, the energy crisis, Three Mile Island, Iranian hostages, a new president shot in 1981, the bombing of our embassy and hundreds of Marines in Lebanon... ."

That list goes on and on and on. He closed his letter by reminding me, "Life is a grindstone ... whether it grinds you down or polishes you up depends on what you are made of."

Another favorite example about perspective hits closer to home. The story goes that a couple received this two-page letter from their 18-year-old daughter during her first year of college:

"I thought I'd let you in on my plans. I have fallen in love with a man who is 40. He is a janitor at my school, and a high-school dropout with two kids. But he is very sweet. I am quitting school to work as a waitress in a bar. I'll let you know if we're getting married once I know for sure if I'm pregnant."

With her eyes filled with tears, the girl's mother began reading page two:

"Relax, Mom and Dad. Nothing I've written is true. No boyfriend, not pregnant, not quitting school. But I am failing math and getting a "C" in Latin. Besides this, I need an increase in my allowance."

The point of her letter? Keep perspective! Sometimes trouble isn't always trouble.

WHAT DO YOU THINK?

6 MORE THOUGHTS FOR YOUR WEEK: PERSPECTIVE

"Our loyalties must transcend our race, our tribe, our class,
and our nation; and this means we must develop a world perspective."
–Martin Luther King Jr.

"When you look at yourself from a universal standpoint, something inside always
reminds or informs you that there are bigger and better things to worry about."
–Albert Einstein

"Wisdom is your perspective on life, your sense of balance, your understanding of how
the various parts and principles apply and relate to each other. It embraces judgment,
discernment, comprehension. It is a gestalt or oneness, an integrated wholeness."
–Stephen R. Covey

"Man is equally incapable of seeing the nothingness from
which he emerges and the infinity in which he is engulfed."
–Blaise Pascal

"I have not failed; I've found 10,000 ways that won't work."
–Thomas Edison

"Bunny slippers remind me of who I am. You can't get a swelled head if you
wear bunny slippers. You can't lose your sense of perspective and start
acting like a star or a rich lady if you keep on wearing bunny slippers.
Besides, bunny slippers give me confidence because they're so jaunty."
–Dean Koontz

■

"A year from now, you may wish you had started today."

–KAREN LAMB
WRITER

I WAS JUST THINKING ABOUT ...
TIME. USE IT WISELY!

If you had a bank that credited your account each morning with $86,400—with no balance carried from day to day—what would you do? Well, you do have such a bank ... time. Every morning it credits you with 86,400 seconds. Every night it rules off as "lost" whatever you have failed to use toward good purposes. It carries over no balances and allows no overdrafts. You can't hoard it, save it, store it, loan it or invest it. You can only use it—time.

There are six terrific truths about time:

First: Nobody can manage time. But you can manage those things that take up your time.

Second: Time is expensive. As a matter of fact, 80 percent of our day is spent on those things or those people that only bring us two percent of our results.

Caught: Infamous Thief

A friend spent his life as a lawman. I loved his stories! A favorite is one he would share with high school and college kids:

Arthur Berry was described by *Time* as "the slickest second-story man in the East," truly one of the most famous jewel thieves of all times. In his years of crime, he committed as many as 150 burglaries and stole jewels valued between $5 and $10 million. He seldom robbed from anyone not listed in the Social Register and often did his work in a tuxedo. On an occasion or two, when caught in the act of a crime by a victim, he charmed his way out of being reported to the police.

Like most people who engage in a life of crime, he was eventually caught, convicted and served 25 years in prison for his crimes. Following his release, he worked as a counterman in a roadside restaurant on the East Coast for $50 a week.

A newspaper reporter found him and interviewed him about his life. After telling about the thrilling episodes of his life he came to the conclusion of the interview saying, "I am not good at morals. But early in my life I was intelligent and clever, and I got along well with people. I think I could have made something of my life, but I didn't. So when you write the story of my life, when you tell people about all the burglaries, don't leave out the biggest one of all.... Don't just tell them I robbed Jesse Livermore, the Wall Street baron or the cousin of the king of England. You tell them Arthur Berry robbed Arthur Berry."

Third: Time is perishable. It cannot be saved for later use.

Fourth: Time is measurable. Everybody has the same amount of time … pauper or king. It is not how much time you have; it is how much you use.

Fifth: Time is irreplaceable. We never make back time once it is gone.

Sixth: Time is a priority. You have enough time for anything in the world, so long as it ranks high enough among your priorities.

Just think about the familiar complaint, "If I just had more time." This is exceedingly self-deceptive! Kings have no more time, beggars no less! God gives to every man 24 golden hours per day. That's 86,400 precious seconds ticking inexorably away.

Here is the point: If you don't manage time, time will manage you.

WHAT DO YOU THINK?

_____

_____

_____

_____

_____

_____

_____

_____

_____

_____

_____

_____

_____

_____

_____

6 MORE THOUGHTS FOR YOUR WEEK: TIME

"Hold fast the time! Guard it, watch over it, every hour, every minute!
Unguarded it slips away like a lizard, smooth, slippery, faithless. Hold
every moment sacred. Give each clarity and meaning, each the weight
of time awareness, each its true and due fulfillment."
–THOMAS MANN

"Time will take your money, but money won't buy time."
–JAMES TAYLOR

"Make use of time if thou lovest eternity. Yesterday cannot
be recalled. Tomorrow cannot be assured. Only today is thine,
which if thou procrastinates thou loses, and if lost, is lost forever.
One today is worth two tomorrows."
–FRANCIS QUARLES

"The future is something which everyone reaches at the rate
of 60 minutes an hour, whatever he does, whoever he is."
–C.S. LEWIS

"For everything there is a season,
And a time for every matter under heaven:
A time to be born, and a time to die;
A time to plant, and a time to pluck up what is planted;
A time to kill, and a time to heal;
A time to break down, and a time to build up;
A time to weep, and a time to laugh;

A time to mourn, and a time to dance;
A time to throw away stones, and a time to gather stones together;
A time to embrace, and a time to refrain from embracing;
A time to seek, and a time to lose;
A time to keep, and a time to throw away;
A time to tear, and a time to sew;
A time to keep silence, and a time to speak,
a time to love, and a time to hate,
A time for war, and a time for peace."

—Ecclesiastes 3:1-8

"We get to think of life as an inexhaustible well. Yet everything happens only a certain number of times, and a very small number, really. How many more times will you remember a certain afternoon of your childhood, some afternoon that's so deeply a part of your being that you can't even conceive of your life without it? Perhaps four or five times more. Perhaps not even that. How many more times will you watch the full moon rise? Perhaps twenty. And yet it all seems limitless."

— Paul Bowles

"Our lives end
the day we
become silent
about the things
that matter."

–MARTIN LUTHER KING JR.
CIVIL RIGHTS LEADER AND CLERGYMAN

I WAS JUST THINKING ABOUT … SPEAKING UP

Demosthenes, one of the greatest Greek orators, spoke out on issues of crucial importance. In his four highly regarded "Philippics," he warned repeatedly about Philip of Macedonia's advance into Greece during the 4th century BC. But first, to rally people with his speeches, he had to deal with a personal handicap … stuttering.

According to the historian Plutarch, Demosthenes had "a perplexed and indistinct utterance and a shortness of breath, which, by breaking and disjointing his sentences much obscured the sense and meaning of what he spoke."

So what did Demosthenes do? He worked on his diction to correct flaws, argued persuasively to restore Athens' supremacy—and took on the hard issues of the day.

As I think about speaking out about controversial or potentially inflammatory issues, and what must be done to be most effective, I recently read this letter exchange that is sad but true.

Dear God,
    Why didn't you save the school children
    in Littleton, Colorado?
Sincerely, Concerned Student

And the reply?
    Dear Concerned Student,
    I am not allowed in schools.
Sincerely, God

Wisdom of Demosthenes

- All speech is vain and empty unless it be accompanied by action.
- As a vessel is known by the sound, whether it be cracked or not, so men are proved, by their speeches, whether they be wise or foolish.
- Small opportunities are often the beginning of great enterprises.

The New School Prayer

Now I sit me down in school, where praying is against the rule.

For this great nation under God, finds mention of Him very odd.

If scripture now the class recites, it violates the Bill of Rights.

And anytime my head I bow becomes a federal matter now.

Our hair can be purple, orange or green—that's no offense. It's the freedom scene.

The law is specific; the law is precise. Prayers spoken aloud are a serious vice.

For praying in a public hall might offend someone with no faith at all.

In silence, alone, we must meditate. God's name is prohibited by the State.

We're allowed to cuss and dress like freaks, pierce our noses, tongues and cheeks.

They've outlawed guns; But FIRST the Bible! To quote the Good Book makes
me liable.

We can elect a pregnant Senior Queen, and make the unwed father Senior King.

It's "inappropriate" to teach right from wrong; we're taught that such "judgments"
don't belong.

We can give out condoms, birth control, study witchcraft, vampires and
totem poles.

But the Ten Commandments are not allowed. No word of God must reach
this crowd.

It's scary here, I must confess. When chaos reigns, the school's a mess.

So, Lord, this silent plea I make: Should I be shot, my soul please take.

Dr. Peter Marshall, the Scottish-American preacher who served as the U.S. Senate Chaplain and author of *A Man Named Peter*, said it best, "The measure of life is not its duration, but its donation." It isn't what you are that matters, or how long your life is, but rather what you do with what you have. Yours can be the tiny voice that makes a difference. You can be that one person who changes history by taking a stand for those principles in which you believe. Isn't it time to speak out for what matters?

6 MORE THOUGHTS FOR YOUR WEEK: SPEAKING UP

"Speak up for those who cannot speak for themselves,
for the rights of all who are destitute."

–Proverbs 31:8

"Go and preach the gospel. Use words, if necessary."

–St. Francis of Assisi

"The only thing necessary for the triumph of evil is for good men to do nothing."

–Edmund Burke

"If you're doing nothing, you're doing wrong."

–Lord Mountbatten

"When Athenians gathered in 399 B.C. to sit in judgment over the 70-year-old, self-proclaimed gadfly Socrates, what they heard was not a plea for forgiveness but a proud, dignified accusation of the verdict. Socrates declared that what he deserved was not the death sentence but rather a reward for attempting to force his fellow citizens to face truth, justice and beauty. In words that would inspire for centuries thereafter, Socrates refused to stoop to a genuine defense of his actions and what he saw as begging for forgiveness and life. He dismissed such an option with the words, 'The difficulty, my friends, is not to avoid death, but to avoid unrighteousness.'"

–Charles Francis

"Even if you're on the right track, you'll get run over if you just sit there."

–Will Rogers

"It takes twenty years to make an overnight success."

–EDDIE CANTOR

SINGER, ACTOR, SONGWRITER

DEFYING THE EXPERTS

So often we defer to the experts, but they aren't always right. With hard work, tenacity and talent, we can prove them wrong! Let me remind you of these ten "expert" opinions:

1. In 1926, Lee deForest, inventor of the cathode ray tube, said, "While theoretically television may be feasible, commercially and financially I consider it an impossibility, a development of which we need waste little time dreaming."

2. In 1943, Thomas Watson, chairman of the board for IBM, said, "I think there is a world market for about five computers."

3. In 1945, Admiral Leahy said about the atomic bomb, "This is the biggest fool thing we've ever done–the bomb will never go off. And I speak as an expert on explosives."

4. Said a recording company executive in 1962 upon turning down the Beatles, "We don't think they will do anything in this market. Guitar groups are on the way out."

5. Written in *BusinessWeek* in 1968, "With over 15 types of foreign cars already on sale here, the Japanese auto industry isn't likely to carve out a big share of the market for itself."

6. Thomas Edison wrote, "Fooling around with alternating currents is just a waste of time. Nobody will use it, ever. It is too dangerous. It could kill a man as quick as a bolt of lightning. Direct current is safe."

7. Napoleon wrote in a letter to Robert Fulton, "What, sir, would you make a ship sail against the wind and currents by lighting a bonfire under her deck? I have no time to listen to such nonsense."

8. An irate banker demanded Alexander Graham Bell remove "that toy" from his office. "That toy" was a telephone.

9. When Margaret Mitchell's Pulitzer Prize-winning book, *Gone with the Wind*, was pitched to a Hollywood producer, he wrote a curt rejection note on the manuscript. Fortunately, moviegoers today can delight in watching eternal heartthrobs Clark Gable and Vivien Leigh!!

10. My favorite: Fred Smith came up with a revolutionary idea for an overnight air-freight service back in 1965 while a student at Yale. He wrote a paper about his new idea for an economics class. His professor called it impractical and gave Fred a "C." Just six years later, Fred put together a business based on his idea. Today the multi-billion-dollar company is in 220 countries and has 290,000 employees and contractors. You know it as Federal Express.

There is a lesson here for us. Chicago architect Daniel Burnham, among the visionaries responsible for the development of the American skyscraper, said it eloquently, "Dream no little dreams for they have no magic to stir men's souls!" The point? Never be the "expert" to tell a dreamer that something cannot be done. God may have been waiting centuries to find the one person willing to trust and follow Him!

"Anything You Can Do…"

Irving Berlin—whose musical compositions, nearly 1,000 in all, ranged from "God Bless America" to "Cheek to Cheek" and "There's No Business Like Show Business"—spent his boyhood as a waiter in Chinatown. He never learned to play, except by ear … and even then, only in F-sharp. Many children today can read music far better than Berlin could. Yet, he wrote the only piece to be included in John Alden Carpenter's collection of the world's greatest music.

Alexander Woollcott knew Berlin well, and his highest tribute to him was this, "He can neither read music nor transcribe it. …He can only give birth to it."

WHAT DO YOU THINK?

_____

_____

_____

_____

6 MORE THOUGHTS FOR YOUR WEEK:
DEFY THE EXPERTS

"The only place you find success before work is in the dictionary."
–MAY V. SMITH

"Most of the world's useful work is done by people who are
pressed for time, or are tired, or don't feel well."
–DOUGLAS SMITHALL FREEMAN

"Chance favors only the prepared mind."
–LOUIS PASTEUR

"Greater than the threat of mighty armies
is an idea whose time has come."
–VICTOR HUGO

"I'm a great believer in luck and I find the harder I work,
the more I have of it."
–THOMAS JEFFERSON

"It's true hard work never killed anybody,
but I figure why take the chance?"
–RONALD REAGAN

■

"Age is an issue of mind over matter. If you don't mind, it doesn't matter."

—MARK TWAIN
AUTHOR AND HUMORIST

I WAS JUST THINKING ABOUT ... AGE

When you think about it, age is really a state of mind! Growing old is no more than a bad habit that a busy person has no time to form!

Dr. George Lawson, a gerontologist, said, "Your mind is still young at 50–your brain doesn't reach its zenith until 10 years after that. And from 60 on, mental efficiency declines very slowly to the age of 80. At 80, you can be just as productive mentally as you were at 30–and you should know a lot more."

"Youth is a circumstance you can't do anything about," wrote architect Frank Lloyd Wright, who was recognized by the American Institute of Architects as the "greatest American architect of all time." He completed the Guggenheim Museum in New York when he was in his nineties. "The trick is to grow up without getting old. It is a spirit, and if it is there after they put you in the box, that's immortality."

Researchers at Stanford studying the lives of 400 famous people found:
- 35 percent of the group's achievements came when they were between 60 and 70.
- 23 percent came between 70 and 80.
- 8 percent came when they were over 80.
- 64 percent of the world's greatest work has been achieved by people over 60.

That's only the beginning! Look at this:
- George Burns won his first Oscar at 80.
- Golda Meir was 71 when she became Prime Minister of Israel.
- Playwright George Bernard Shaw broke his leg at 96. He was trimming a tree in his backyard.
- Michelangelo was 71 when he painted the Sistine Chapel.
- Albert Schweitzer was still performing surgery in an African hospital at 89.
- Casey Stengel didn't retire from managing the New York Mets until he was 75.

- Alexander Graham Bell perfected the telephone at 58, and he solved the problem of stabilizing the balance in airplanes in his 70s.
- John Wesley, who built the Methodist Church at 83, was annoyed that at 86, he could not preach more than twice a day and that he could not write more than 15 hours without his eyes hurting. He complained of his increasing tendency to lie in bed until 5:30 in the morning!

Then there was the lady who began painting at 78 years. You might find this amazing because she never had a lesson or had even been in an art gallery. With only a few months of schooling, she had lived 50 years of her life as a hired girl on a farm. When she began painting at 78, she had to do so while dealing with arthritis. When she was 88 years of age, she was among some of the best-known artists in the world. When she reached 90, she had pictures hanging in galleries worldwide. When she reached 100 years of age, birthday greetings from all over the world came to her. In fact, four living ex-presidents of the United States wrote greetings to her. She died in 1961 at 101 years of age. Every major paper in the country carried stories about and pictures of her. Heads of state worldwide sent condolences.

The painter's name? Grandma Moses.

When asked how she decided to become a painter, she said, "I decided to quit existing and start living." In other words, she got a goal for her life. Try as I might, I cannot get away from the fact that those who want to make a life as well as make a living are those who take the time to decide who they are, what they want to be and how they plan to get there.

Age really is a state of mind! Satchel Paige, one of the greatest pitchers in baseball, once said, "How old would you be if you didn't know how old you were?"

WHAT DO YOU THINK?

_____

_____

_____

_____

6 MORE THOUGHTS FOR YOUR WEEK: AGE

"It is never too late to be who you might have been."

–GEORGE ELIOT

"And in the end, it's not the years in your life that count.
It's the life in your years."

–ABRAHAM LINCOLN

"I'm not interested in age. People who tell me their age are silly.
You're as old as you feel."

–ELIZABETH ARDEN

"The first half of our lives is ruined by our parents,
and the second half by our children."

–CLARENCE DARROW

"The great thing about getting older is that you don't
lose all the other ages you've been."

–MADELEINE L'ENGLE

"You don't stop laughing because you grow old;
you grow old because you stop laughing."

–MICHAEL PRITCHARD

"Adversity has the effect of eliciting talents, which in prosperous circumstances would have lain dormant."

—HORACE
ROMAN POET

THE "UP" SIDE OF ADVERSITY

Remember cooking expert Julia Child? One night she decided to make soufflé, and she mixed this and that together, dropping things on the floor. Finally she took the soufflé and tossed it in the oven. After letting it bake awhile, she announced, "Now it's ready!" But when she opened the oven door, the soufflé fell flat as a pancake. She just smiled and said, "Well, you can't win them all. Bon appétit!"

I love people like that! To them, failure is never final. Sometimes the greatest inventions come from major mistakes—Kellogg's Corn Flakes resulted from boiled wheat being left in a baking pan overnight. Ivory Soap floats because a batch was left in the mixer too long, getting a large volume of air whipped into it.

The point? It takes no talent to be a quitter. That's why Lord Byron wrote, "Adversity is the first path to truth."

Restauranteur Wolfgang Puck said, "I learned more from the one restaurant that didn't work than from all the ones that were successful." He now owns five critically acclaimed restaurants in California alone, as well as locations in Chicago, Las Vegas and Tokyo.

And here's one of my favorite stories about the upside of adversity. Lou Little, the famous Columbia University football coach, loved to tell about a teenager who lived alone with his father. The young man was on the high school football team, and although he never left the bench, his father never missed a game. He was always in the stands, cheering on the team. After high school, the young man went on to college and tried out as a "walk-on." Everyone was sure he wouldn't make it. But against all odds, he did ... because of his determination. But the coach never put him in to play during a single game—not even for a single down.

At one of the last practices before the big play-off game at the end of the last season, the coach met him on the field holding a telegram. The young man read it, and the color drained from his face. "My father died this morning. Do you think it'd be all right if I missed practice today?" he asked.

The coach put his arm gently around the young man's shoulders and said, "Son, take the rest of the week off. In fact, don't worry about coming back for the game Saturday." On Saturday, the game was not going well, however. During the third quarter, when his team was down by ten, the young man quietly appeared on the sidelines. The coach and his fellow teammates were astounded. Almost immediately the young man approached the coach with pleas to play. But the coach pretended not to hear. There was no way he was going to put in the weakest player on the team. The young man persisted, and finally, the coach gave in because he felt sorry for all the kid had been through.

Reviresco, a Word to Remember
While reading a magazine on a flight to San Francisco, I came across a picture of a dead tree stump out of which grew a small green shoot. The picture was titled "Reviresco". I later learned that this is a Latin word meaning, "I flourish in adversity."
–*It's Always Too Soon to Quit*

Within minutes of the young man taking the field, no one could believe their eyes. He ran, he passed, he blocked and tackled like a star! In the closing seconds of the game, this kid intercepted a pass and ran all the way back for the winning touchdown. The fans broke loose! His teammates hoisted him to their shoulders! Such cheering and joy!

"Kid, I can't believe it," said the coach. "You were fantastic! How did you do it? What got into you?"

With tears in his eyes, the young man replied, "Coach, I know you knew my dad had died, but did you know he was blind?" The coach shook his head. "Well, today I was able to play better than ever because even though Dad came to every game, today was the first time he could see me play."

6 MORE THOUGHTS FOR YOUR WEEK: ADVERSITY

"What a testing of character adversity is!"
–HARRY EMERSON FOSDICK

"Every adversity, every failure, every heartache carries
with it the seed of an equal or greater benefit."
- NAPOLEON HILL

"In the middle of difficulty lies opportunity."
–ALBERT EINSTEIN

"Gray skies are just clouds passing over."
–DUKE ELLINGTON

"God doesn't always smooth the path,
but sometimes He puts springs in the wagon."
–MARSHALL LUCAS

"The way I see it, if you want the rainbow,
you gotta put up with the rain."
–DOLLY PARTON

■

"Doubts are
the ants in the
pants of faith.
They keep it awake
and moving."

—FREDERICK BUECHNER
AMERICAN WRITER AND THEOLOGIAN

I WAS JUST THINKING ABOUT … OUR DOUBTS

Life really is all in how you look at it. Just think about these twelve truths:

1. You say, "But it is impossible!"
   God says, "All things are possible." (Luke 18:27)

2. You say, "I'm too tired."
   God says, "I will give you rest." (Matthew 11:28-30)

3. You say, "Nobody really loves me."
   God says, "I love you." (John 3:16)

4. You say, "But I can't go on."
   God says, "My grace is sufficient." (II Corinthians 12:9)

5. You say, "I just can't figure things out."
   God says, "I will direct your steps." (Proverbs 3:5-6)

6. You say, "I can't do it."
   God says, "You can do all things." (Philippians 4:13)

7. You say, "I can't forgive myself."
   God says, "I forgive you." (I John 1:9)

8. You say, "I can't manage."
   God says, "I will supply all your needs." (Philippians 4:19)

9. You say, "I am afraid."
    God says, "I have not given you a spirit of fear." (II Timothy 1:7)

10. You say, "I don't have enough faith."
    God says, "I've given everyone a measure of faith." (Romans 12:3)

11. You say, "I'm not smart enough."
    God says, "I give you wisdom." (I Corinthians 1:30)

12. You say, "I feel all alone."
    God says, "I will never leave you or forsake you." (Hebrews 13:5)

Many of us talk about faith, but somehow we have a problem really knowing what we have faith in. Two examples:

Henry Edward Cardinal Manning (1808-1892) began his ministry in the Anglican Church, but after his conversion to Catholicism, he became Archbishop of Westminster and a popular writer. During a period of great depression and darkening of his faith, he went into a well-known bookstore for a copy of one of his own books, *Faith in God.* As he was waiting for the book to be sent up from the storeroom, supposedly a man's voice called up, "Manning's *Faith in God* is all gone."

That brings to mind a funny story often told by Reverend Emmett Fox, a spiritual leader who was influential in the founding of Alcoholics Anonymous. It seems he had a visit from a woman who had heard him talk on building faith. After she heard his talk, she went out to Macy's in New York and charged a lot of expensive merchandise to her account. Eventually, Macy's began to press her for payment on the bill. It was then she went to see Dr. Fox again. "But I had faith—I stepped out on faith," she told him. "You didn't step out on faith," Dr. Fox replied. "You stepped out on Macy's."

Put your doubts aside. Trust God to bring you through the tough times. And always remember the words of Shakespeare who said it best, "Our doubts are traitors, and make us lose the good we oft might win, by fearing to attempt."

WHAT DO YOU THINK?

6 MORE THOUGHTS FOR YOUR WEEK: DOUBTS

"If you must tell me your opinions, tell me what you believe in.
I have plenty of doubts of my own."

–JOHANN WOLFGANG VON GOETHE

"One must verify or expel his doubts,
and convert them into the certainty of YES or NO."

–THOMAS CARLYLE

"Don't waste life in doubts and fears; spend yourself on the work before
you, well assured that the right performance of this hour's duties will be
the best preparation for the hours and ages that will follow it."

–RALPH WALDO EMERSON

"Faith believes in spite of the circumstances
and acts in spite of the consequences."

–ADRIAN ROGERS

"The deplorable mania of doubt exhausts me.
I doubt about everything, even my doubts."

–GUSTAVE FLAUBERT

"The beginning of wisdom is found in doubting; by doubting we come to
the question, and by seeking we may come upon the truth."

–PIERRE ABELARD

■

"If you don't know where you are going, you'll end up someplace else."

—YOGI BERRA
YANKEE MANAGER AND CATCHER

I WAS JUST THINKING ABOUT ... HUMOR

I wrote my second book with Yogi Berra in mind. History proves that our greatest days are still to be had, our greatest dreams have yet to be realized, if we will commit to memory six simple words: *It's Always Too Soon to Quit!* Those words became the title of my second book. During Berra's 19 years with the Yankees, he appeared in 14 World Series, winning ten championships—and he always used HUMOR.

A master of malapropisms, this Baseball Hall of Famer once remarked, "I really didn't say everything I said." Some people think Yogi is dumb because he gave us so many sayings designed to make us laugh:

"A nickel ain't worth a dime anymore."
"Good pitching beats good hitting every time—and vice-versa."
"Baseball is 90 percent half mental. It ain't over till it's over."
"This is like déjà vu all over again."
"When you come to a fork in the road, take it."
"We made too many wrong mistakes."
"It ain't the heat, it's the humility."

Truth is, Yogi is a very smart man. My favorite Berra-ism is "What a sorry old world this would be if it was always winter ... and never Christmas." That came on the heels of Yogi's most famous quote, "The Opry ain't over till the fat lady sings."

WHAT DO YOU THINK?

_____

_____

_____

6 MORE THOUGHTS FOR YOUR WEEK: HUMOR

"Don't get your knickers in a knot.
Nothing is solved, and it just makes you walk funny."

–KATHRYN CARPENTER

"Clothes make the man. Naked people have little or
no influence on society."

–MARK TWAIN

"Too bad the only people who know how to run
the country are busy driving cabs and cutting hair."

–GEORGE BURNS

"No day is so bad that it can't be fixed with a nap."

–CARRIE SNOW

"A bank is a place that will lend you money
if you can prove that you don't need it."

–BOB HOPE

"She's the kind of girl who climbed the ladder of success wrong by wrong."

–MAE WEST

■

"People may doubt what you say, but they will always believe what you do."

–LEWIS CASS
MILITARY OFFICER AND POLITICIAN

I WAS JUST THINKING ABOUT ... GOD AGAIN

How blessed I am that God has given me so much. One thing that I appreciate most is that I have a Sunday school class full of people who love and pray for me. In the mail, I received the following "15 Things That God Won't Ask" from one of those wonderful people. I thought it was so outstanding that I wanted to share it with you.

15 Things That God Won't Ask

1. God won't ask what kind of car you drove, but how many people with no transportation you drove.

2. God won't ask the square footage of your house, but how many people you welcomed into it.

3. God won't ask about the fancy clothes you had in your closet, but how many of those clothes helped the needy.

4. God won't ask about your social status, but what kind of class you displayed.

5. God won't ask how many material possessions you had, but if they dictated your life.

6. God won't ask your highest salary, but if you compromised your character to achieve it.

7. God won't ask how much overtime you worked, but if you worked overtime for your friends and family.

8. God won't ask how many promotions you received, but how you promoted others.

9. God won't ask what your job title was, but if you performed that job to the best of your ability.

10. God won't ask what you did to help yourself, but what you did to help others.

11. God won't ask how many friends you had, but if you were a true friend to those in your life.

12. God won't ask what you did to protect your rights, but what you did to protect others.

13. God won't ask in what neighborhood you lived, but how you treated your neighbors.

14. God won't ask about the color of your skin, but the content of your character.

15. God won't ask if your deeds matched your words, but how many times they didn't.

WHAT DO YOU THINK?

---

6 MORE THOUGHTS FOR YOUR WEEK: GOD

"God gives us the ingredients for our daily bread,
but he expects us to do the baking."
—WILLIAM ARTHUR WARD

"What is the greatest thought that has ever passed through your head?"
someone asked Daniel Webster. He answered, "My accountability to God."
—DANIEL WEBSTER

"I have held many things in my hands, and I have lost them all; but
whatever I have placed in God's hands, that I still possess."
—MARTIN LUTHER

"People see God every day; they just don't recognize him."
—PEARL BAILEY

"When we can't piece together the puzzle of our own lives, remember the
best view of a puzzle is from above. Let Him help put you together."
—AMETHYST SNOW-RIVERS

"God enters by a private door into every individual."
—RALPH WALDO EMERSON

■

"Happiness is the realization of God in the heart. Happiness is the result of praise and thanksgiving, of faith, of acceptance; a quiet, tranquil realization of the love of God."

—WHITE EAGLE

PAWNEE CHIEF

I WAS JUST THINKING ABOUT … MEDITATION

The best way to move ahead is often by looking back. For years, I've made it a practice to find a quiet time to reflect. It helps me see how blessed I am, how far I've come and, in spite of mistakes and missteps, it gives me ideas of how to best move forward.

One of the ways I prepare for the future is to read the following list of things I am thankful for:

- For a family that lifts me when I'm low, loves me when I'm unlovable and makes me believe that I am the man they think I am.
- For hours of despair, loneliness and heartache that have tried my manhood and not found me wanting.
- For friends who "know me and like me anyway," who encourage me by their trust, who accept me by their actions and who keep my feet on firm foundations.
- For the joy of competition in the business arena, the thrill of victory and the courage to see defeat as a lesson to make me stronger.
- For clients whose beliefs are inspiring, whose concern for their customers is encouraging, whose compassion for their employees is enriching and whose success in the business world is transferable.
- For a land where all are welcome, everyone is equal and success is a promise, not a platitude.
- For a God whose presence is personal, whose care is certain, whose promise is dependable and whose love is explainable.
- For a nation whose beliefs are tested, whose laws are followed and whose values are inspiring.

- For a church where God is love, whose members are humble and whose witness is everlasting.

Med-i-ta-tion, even the sound of the word, when repeated, has a quiet, steadiness to it. Consider these wise words on self-reflection from Swiss-born psychiatrist Elisabeth Kubler-Ross: "In Switzerland I was educated in line with the basic premise: work, work, work. You are only a valuable human being if you work. This is utterly wrong. Half-working, half-dancing—that is the right mixture. I myself have danced and played too little." At another occasion, she said, "There is no need to go to India or anywhere else to find peace. You will find that deep place of silence right in your room, your garden or even your bathtub."

WHAT DO YOU THINK?

_____

_____

_____

_____

_____

_____

_____

_____

_____

_____

_____

_____

_____

_____

_____

_____

_____

6 MORE THOUGHTS FOR YOUR WEEK: MEDITATION

"The cyclone derives its powers from a calm center. So does a person."

–Norman Vincent Peale

"If I always appear prepared, it is because before entering an undertaking,
I have meditated long and have foreseen what might occur. It is not genius
where reveals to me suddenly and secretly what I should do in circumstances
unexpected by others; it is thought and preparation."

–Napoleon Bonaparte

"Reading makes a full man, meditation
a profound man, discourse a clear man."

–Benjamin Franklin

"God speaks to each of us in the beauty of every flower,
in the grace of every tree, in the shimmer of every star."

–Carolyn Hoppe

"Soon silence will have passed into legend. Man has turned his back on silence.
Day after day he invents machines and devices that increase noise and distract
humanity from the essence of life, contemplation, meditation."

–Jean Arp

"Follow effective action with quiet reflection.
From the quiet reflection will come even more effective action."

–Peter Drucker

"Those who say
it cannot be
done should not
interrupt the
person doing it."

–Chinese Proverb

AN EXPRESSION, "AND THEN SOME"

A man was pursuing a dream, but in order to make that dream come true, he needed capital. He went to over 300 banks and they all said, "No."

Disgusted and depressed, he went home for lunch one day and as he sat down, his wife put a note by his plate. The note had only three words, "And Then Some." Give it all you've got, and then some! SO the man went out and visited his 302nd bank. Lo and behold, they said, "YES." Walt Disney now had the capital he needed because he did all he could do … and then some!

And how else can you explain this story? A small middle-aged lady from Montgomery, AL, one day decided that she, too, was a human, and therefore, she had every right to a seat on the bus. That day Rosa Parks decided to take a stand and refused to give up her seat simply because she was black. Although frightened of what might happen as a result of her courageous stand, Parks refused to be bullied into being something less than she was. Her courage and fortitude set off a civil rights movement that changed the course of history for an entire race of people. Rosa Parks had made a difference.

The point of this story is there is greatness in everyone. The difference between the great and the mediocre, the powerful and the weak, the remembered and the forgotten is to give it all you've got—and then some!

Just think about the power of words. When spoken by a man or a woman who has the power of belief and the benefit of experience, we can hear words that change our lives. How well do I remember Professor Richard Weaver II of Bowling Green State University when he said:

"A prominent salesman friend of mine summed up his success in three simple words: 'and then some.' He discovered at an early age that most of the differences between average people and top people could be explained in those three words.

"The top people did what was expected of them ... AND THEN SOME. They were thoughtful to others, kind and considerate ... AND THEN SOME. They met their obligations and responsibilities fairly and squarely ... AND THEN SOME. They were good friends to the people in their lives ... AND THEN SOME. They could be counted on in an emergency ... AND THEN SOME."

And then some... three little words, and those three little words could transform our society. It could become a philosophy of life, a way of living.

WHAT DO YOU THINK?

The Ten Most Powerful Two-Letter Words:
If it is to be, it is up to me.

6 MORE THOUGHTS FOR YOUR WEEK:
GIVING 110 PERCENT

"The average person puts only 25 percent of his energy and ability into his work.
The world takes off its hat to those who put in more than 50 percent of their capacity,
and stands on its head for those few and far between souls who devote 100 percent."

–ANDREW CARNEGIE

"Good enough never is."

–DEBBI FIELDS

"Folks who never do any more than they are paid
for never get paid for any more than they do."

–ELBERT HUBBARD

"A life spent in making mistakes is not only more honorable,
but more useful than a life spent doing nothing."

–GEORGE BERNARD SHAW

"It's never crowded along the extra mile."

–WAYNE DYER

"The riders in a race do not stop short when they reach the goal. There is a
little finishing canter before coming to a standstill. There is time to hear
the kind voice of friends and to say to one's self: 'The work is done.'"

–OLIVER WENDELL HOLMES

"**Every man is enthusiastic** at times. One **man** has enthusiasm for thirty minutes, another **man** has it for thirty days. But it **is** the **man** who has it for thirty years who makes a success in life."

–EDWARD B. BUTLER

AMERICAN BUSINESSMAN

I WAS JUST THINKING ABOUT... ENTHUSIASM

One night the fire department of a small West Texas town raced to the outskirts of town where they found the local Baptist church engulfed in flames. People came from all over town either to help fight the flames or to watch the burning church that most of them attended. They watched in sadness as their church slowly disintegrated before their eyes.

As the pastor scanned the faces in the crowd, he caught sight of a young man standing off to one side away from the crowd. The pastor had not seen this man before, so he walked over to introduce himself. "I'm the pastor of this church," he said, as he extended his hand in friendly greeting. "I don't think I've ever seen you at this church before." "Preacher," the man responded, "this church has never been on fire before!"

This story reminds me of the power of enthusiasm! Couple it with goals and you have a winning scenario.

I am reminded of the high school kid with a serious weight problem—he weighed 268 pounds. In spite of his weight, he became a successful model and actor. You may remember him as one of the first men to wear the grapes in the Fruit of the Loom commercials.

In spite of his relative success, he did not feel good about himself. One day, he found a note on his car, "Fat people die young. Please don't die." –An Admirer

This young man went on a crash diet and in three months lost over 100 pounds ... mostly by starvation. The result? He wrecked his body. He became dehydrated, he lost his hair, and he suffered many other health problems that finally resulted in his hospitalization.

While he was recovering, he wrote a goal: To learn how to lose weight safely through good nutrition and proper exercise. After he learned this, he wanted to share his knowledge with others troubled by obesity. He was so enthusiastic about his new knowledge that people immediately were attracted to him. He eventually made weight-loss education his business.

Today, Richard Simmons is recognized all over this world, even appearing on *Saturday Night Live*. But he could not have done it without a goal that changed his life—and enormous ENTHUSIASM.

WHAT DO YOU THINK?

_____

_____

_____

_____

_____

_____

_____

_____

_____

_____

_____

_____

_____

_____

_____

_____

_____

_____

_____

_____

_____

6 MORE THOUGHTS FOR YOUR WEEK: ENTHUSIASM

"Enthusiasm is the electricity of life. How do you get it?
You act enthusiastic until you make it a habit."
–GORDON PARKS

"Enthusiasm is at the bottom of all progress!
With it, there is accomplishment. Without it, there are only alibis."
–HENRY FORD

"I think fanaticism is underrated. I'm a fanatic about the engineering
groups. Steve [Jobs] is a fanatic about the user experience and design,
and it clearly has made a huge difference for Apple that he says that it
all has to come together ... a holistic view."
–BILL GATES

"If you are not fired with enthusiasm, you will be fired with enthusiasm."
–VINCE LOMBARDI

Norman Vincent Peale said, "Throw your heart over the fence and the rest
will follow" and he also believed: "Think excitement, talk excitement, act out
excitement and you are bound to become an excited person. Life will take on
a new zest, deeper interest and greater meaning."
–NORMAN VINCENT PEALE

"Joy is not in things; it is in us."
–RICHARD WAGNER

"Behind me is infinite power. Before me is endless possibility. Around me is boundless opportunity. Why should I fear?"

—STELLA STUART
WRITER

I WAS JUST THINKING ABOUT ... FEAR

There is a horrible and deadly disease—fear! Fear is the basis for most superstitions. Superstitious people will not walk under ladders, allow black cats to cross their paths, or leave their homes on Friday the 13th for fear of bad luck! But fear has much more severe effects on people than the development of little superstitious habits. ...

Paul Parker said, "Fear is the most devastating of all human emotions. Man has no trouble like the paralyzing effects of fear." Throughout the Scriptures we find references that indicate that fear is unhealthy. The Bible states over 350 times that we must "fear not." Yet, we heed not.

So what is fear? Most psychologists agree that it is "holding mental pictures of what I don't want to happen." Maybe that's what Mark Twain meant when he said, "I'm an old man and have known a great many troubles, but most of them never happened." And don't forget that Dr. Will James, the pioneering American psychologist and philosopher, was the first to identify the Law of Self-Fulfilling Prophecy, which states: *Be careful of what you expect because you are probably going to get it!*

Fear and stress take a phenomenal toll on the health and lives of people who allow it to control them. If you tell yourself each day that you can't handle a specific job, that you'll never make it, that you're destined to be a "nobody," then that is exactly what will happen. The subconscious mind believes what it is told, so it will cause you to act in a way as to bring about the very things you fear! If you program your mind negatively, it will translate into your body. You will have headaches, backaches, ulcers and other physical ailments.

On the other hand, if you program your mind positively, you will increase your capacity for living. Winners are never surprised to win because they *expect* to win! They dwell on the positive aspects of every situation. But how do they do that?

They trust in a God who loves them and wants the best for them. They believe, just like President Truman did, in His promise of power found in Jeremiah 29:11,

"For I know the plans I have for you," declared the Lord, "plans for your welfare and not for calamity to give you a future and a hope."

Believe in God ... believe in yourself ... expect the best! If fear knocks on your door, let Jesus answer!

WHAT DO YOU THINK?

6 MORE THOUGHTS FOR YOUR WEEK: FEAR

"Never let the fear of striking out get in your way."

–BABE RUTH

"Taking a new step, uttering a new word, is what people fear most."

–FYODOR DOSTOYEVSKY

"Fear has a large shadow, but he himself is small."

–RUTH GENDLER

"You miss 100 percent of the shots you don't take."

–WAYNE GRETZKY

FEAR (unknown author):
F - False
E - Evidence
A - Appearing
R - Real

"Fear is that little darkroom where negatives are developed."

–MICHAEL PRITCHARD

■

"You must do the thing you think you cannot do."

—ELEANOR ROOSEVELT
First Lady, Activist and Author

I WAS JUST THINKING ABOUT … COURAGE.

Our nation has never known a moment when it had a greater need of courage! Here is the question—What exactly is courage?

Author, medical missionary, explorer and European discoverer of Victoria Falls, Dr. David Livingstone, spent most of his adult life living in primitive conditions in Africa. Although tiresome, fatiguing and dangerous, Dr. Livingstone's work was to him a labor of love.

In Africa, Dr. Livingstone received a letter from some well-meaning friends that read, "We would like to send other men to you. Have you found a good road into your area yet?"

Dr. Livingstone sent this message in reply: "If you have men who will only come if they know there is a good road, I don't want them. I want strong, courageous men who will come if there is no road at all."

An ancient proverb reminds us, "Courage consists not so much in avoiding danger as in conquering it."

Remember the story of the man who stood before God, his heart breaking from the pain, injustice and fear in the world. "Dear God," he cried. "Look at our world. … Why don't you send us help?"

God replied, "I did send help. I sent you."

What Is Courage?

- Courage is mastering our fears and getting on with the wonderful things life has to offer—even when it appears there is no road on which to travel.
- Courage is flourishing in adversity and facing life's disappointments head-on.
- Courage is not allowing fear to take over and control our lives. It is making plans for ways to overcome those fears.
- Courage is accepting the responsibilities that it would be more comfortable not to accept.
- Courage is performing the task that it would be easier not to do.
- Courage is taking the least traveled path.

6 MORE THOUGHTS FOR YOUR WEEK: COURAGE

"Courage is the ladder on which all the other virtues mount."
—CLARE BOOTH LUCE

"One man with courage makes a majority."
—ANDREW JACKSON

"Courage is fear that has said its prayers."
—DOROTHY BERNARD

"Courage without conscience is a wild beast."
—ROBERT G. INGERSOLL

"One isn't necessarily born with courage, but one is born with potential.
Without courage, we cannot practice any other virtue with consistency.
We can't be kind, true, merciful, generous, or honest."
—MAYA ANGELOU

"When a resolute young fellow steps up to the great bully, the world, and takes
him boldly by the beard, he is often surprised to find it comes off in his hand,
and that it was only tied on to scare away the timid adventurers."
—RALPH WALDO EMERSON

■

"It's kind of fun to do the impossible."

–WALT DISNEY
DREAMER, CREATOR, IMAGINEER

DOING THE "IMPOSSIBLE"

I heard a story in church recently. The preacher was talking about Moses and the Exodus. That story led me to do a bit of research, and just look what I found:

Moses and the people were in the desert, but what was he going to do with them? They had to be fed, and feeding two or three million people requires a lot of food! According to the Quartermaster General in the Army, Moses would need 1,500 tons of food each day. In order to bring that much food each day, two freight trains, each a mile long, would be necessary!

Not only that, but while they were out in the desert, they would need firewood for cooking the food. This would take 4,000 tons of wood—or three freight trains, each a mile long! And they had to do this for 40 years!

Oh yes, and they would need water. If they only had enough to drink and wash a few dishes, it would take 11 million gallons each day … a tank car 1,800 miles long is needed to move that amount of water!

And then there's another thing. They had to cross the Red Sea in one night. If they went on a narrow path, double file, the line would be 800 miles long, requiring 35 days and nights to get across the water. There had to have been a space in the Red Sea three miles wide in order to allow the people to cross 5,000 abreast to get over in one night.

A Catchy Idea: Do the Impossible

Johnny loved football. He played every chance he got, and his dreams became reality when he played for St. Justin High School in Pittsburgh. He tried to make the Notre Dame team, but deemed too small, he settled for playing at a smaller college. Upon graduation, he tried to play for the Pittsburgh Steelers, but he was cut. Johnny worked construction and played some amateur football … all while staying in touch with every NFL team. All he wanted was a chance. He never gave up. The Baltimore Colts responded, and he soon became one of the top quarterbacks in the league, leading the Colts to a world championship.

Ultimately Johnny Unitas–who did the IMPOSSIBLE–was inducted into the Football Hall of Fame.

But there was another problem too! Each time they camped, a campground two-thirds the size of Rhode Island (roughly 750 square miles) was required. Just for nightly camping!

Do you think Moses figured all this out before he left Egypt? I think not! You see, Moses believed in God ... and that God could take care of these things for him.

Now do you think God has any trouble taking care of your needs? Life's biggest secret seems to be, "Never Give Up!" As Nelson Mandela says, "It always seems impossible until it's done."

WHAT DO YOU THINK?

6 MORE THOUGHTS FOR YOUR WEEK:
DOING THE IMPOSSIBLE

"Start by doing what is necessary, then what's possible, and suddenly you are doing the impossible."

–St. Francis of Assisi

"I am always doing that which I cannot do, in order that I may learn how to do it."

–Pablo Picasso

"Science fiction, you're right, it's crazy. You wanna hear something really nutty? I heard of a couple of guys who wanna build something called an airplane."

–Victor Grippi

"I tell you the truth, if you have faith as small as a mustard seed, you can say to this mountain, 'Move from here to there' and it will move. Nothing will be impossible to you."

–Matthew 17:20-21

"Sometimes I've believed as many as six impossible things before breakfast."

–Lewis Carroll

"When you believe and think 'I can,' you activate your motivation, commitment, confidence, concentration, excitement—all of which relate directly to achievement."

– Dr. Jerry Lynch

■

"Gratitude is the key to happiness."

–C.S. LEWIS

I WAS JUST THINKING ABOUT …

GIVING THANKS

Recently I received an e-mail about a letter from a paralyzed veteran to his unborn child. I read the letter several times and realized how each of us sometimes ignores all the blessings God has so generously showered upon us—whether it be the family we have, the good health we have, the financial blessings we have or even the church we have.

Take a moment to read this letter, which still takes my breath away:

Son –

Your mother is very special. Few men know what it's like to receive appreciation for taking their wives out to dinner when it entails what it does for us. It means she has to dress me, shave me, brush my teeth, comb my hair, wheel me out of the house and down the steps, open the garage, put me in the car, go around to the other side of the car, start it up, back it out, get out of the car, close the garage, get back in the car, and drive to the restaurant.

Then it starts all over again; she gets out of the car, unfolds the wheelchair, opens the door, spins me around, stands me up, seats me in the wheelchair, pushes the pedals out, closes the door and locks the car, wheels me into the restaurant, then takes the pedals off the wheelchair so I won't be uncomfortable. We sit down to have dinner, and she feeds me throughout the entire meal. When it's over, she pays the bill, pushes the wheelchair out to the car again and reverses the same routine. When it's all over, she says with true warmth, "Honey, thank you for taking me out to dinner." I never quite know what to say.

–Dad

With all the soldiers injured in Iraq and Afghanistan, the paralyzed veteran could have easily been someone in our family or a neighbor's family, and his sense of thankfulness awakens us to the blessings in our own lives.

WHAT DO YOU THINK?

_____

_____

_____

_____

_____

_____

_____

_____

_____

_____

_____

_____

_____

_____

_____

_____

_____

_____

_____

_____

_____

_____

6 MORE THOUGHTS FOR YOUR WEEK:

GIVING THANKS

"Appreciate everything your associates do for the business. Nothing else can quite substitute for a few well-chosen, well-timed, sincere words of praise. They're absolutely free and worth a fortune."

–SAM WALTON

"If the only prayer you said in your whole life was, 'thank you,' that would suffice."

–MEISTER ECKHART

"For each new morning with its light, For rest and shelter of the night, For health and food, for love and friends, For everything Thy goodness sends."

–RALPH WALDO EMERSON

"As we express our gratitude, we must never forget that the highest appreciation is not to utter words, but to live by them."

–JOHN F. KENNEDY

"I learned to love the journey, not the destination. I learned that this is not a dress rehearsal, and that today is the only guarantee you get. Consider the lilies of the field. Look at the fuzz on a baby's ear. Read in the backyard with the sun on your face. Learn to be happy. And think of life as a terminal illness, because, if you do, you will live it with joy and passion, as it ought to be lived."

–ANNA QUINDLEN

"When you give yourself, you receive more than you give."

–ANTOINE DE SAINT-EXUPERY

■

"Teaching kids to count is fine, but teaching them what counts is best."

BOB TALBERT
JOURNALIST

OUR ROLE AS TEACHERS

Maybe we're NOT teaching our kids the right things! A friend sent me the following "8 Rules Our Kids (and Grandkids) Should Learn." All of us are teachers, whether we realize it or not, called upon every day to share what we know. Read these rules and share the wisdom.

Rule 1: Life is not fair … get used to it.

Rule 2: You will NOT make $75,000 a year right out of high school. You won't be vice president until you learn Rule 1.

Rule 3: If you think your teacher is tough, wait until you have a boss. He doesn't have tenure.

Rule 4: Flipping burgers is not beneath your dignity. Your grand-parents had a different word for burger-flipping … opportunity.

Rule 5: Before you were born, your parents weren't as boring as they are now. They got that way from paying

ABCs of Clear Communication

Everybody but John had signed up for a new company pension plan that required a small employee contribution. The company paid all the rest. Unfortunately, 100 percent employee participation was required—otherwise the plan was off.

John's boss and his fellow workers pleaded with him over and over again, but to no avail. John said that the plan would never pay off.

Finally, the company's president called John into his office for a meeting. The president said, "John, here is a copy of the new pension plan, and here is a pen. I want you to sign it, or you are fired."

John immediately signed the papers.

When asked why he hadn't signed earlier, John simply replied, "Nobody had explained it to me so clearly before."

your bills, cleaning your clothes and listening to you talk about how cool you are. So before you save the rainforest from the parasites of your parents' generation, try delousing the closet in your own room.

Rule 6: Life is not divided into semesters. You don't get summers off, and very few employers are interested in helping you "find yourself." Do that on your own time!

Rule 7: Television is NOT real life. In real life people have to leave the coffee shop and go to work.

Rule 8: Be nice to nerds. Chances are, you will end up working for one.

WHAT DO YOU THINK?

6 MORE THOUGHTS FOR YOUR WEEK: TEACHING

"Each second we live is a new and unique moment of the universe, a moment that will never be again. And what do we teach our children? We teach them that two and two make four, and that Paris is the capital of France. When will we also teach them what they are? We should say to each of them: Do you know what you are? You are a marvel. You are unique. In all the years that have passed, there has never been another child like you. Your legs, your arms, your clever fingers, the way you move. You may become a Shakespeare, a Michelangelo, a Beethoven. You have the capacity for anything. Yes, you are a marvel. And when you grow up, can you then harm another who is, like you, a marvel? You must work, we must all work, to make the world worthy of its children."

–PABLO CASALS

"You learn to speak by speaking, to study by studying, to run by running, to work by working; in just the same way you learn to love by loving."

–ST. FRANCIS DE SALES

"Experience: that most brutal of teachers. But you learn, my God, do you learn."

–C.S. LEWIS

"We learn as much from sorrow as from joy, as much from illness as from health, from handicap as much as from advantage—and indeed perhaps more."

–PEARL S. BUCK

"A poor surgeon hurts one person at a time. A poor teacher hurts 30."

–ERNEST BOYER

"The mediocre teacher tells; the good teacher explains; the superior teacher demonstrates; the great teacher inspires."

–WILLIAM ARTHUR WARD

■

"Challenge is
a dragon with
a gift in its mouth.
Tame the dragon,
and the gift
is yours."

—NOELA EVANS
WRITER

AMAZING TURNAROUNDS

Challenges and obstacles can cripple us—coping with a daunting situation at home, or at work. But there's something to be said for the take-the-bull-by-the-horns approach (or the dragon, as referenced in writer Noela Evans' quote) and turn around the situation … decisively.

One of my favorite examples of a turnaround comes from business. In 1985, Jan Carlson had just been named CEO of Scandinavian Airlines, a company deeply in trouble. They had just been ranked by a consumer poll as the worst airline in the world. Last in service, last in dependability and last in profits as a percentage of sales. Then just one year later in the same poll, they were ranked number one in all three categories. How did they do that?

By focusing on the most critical issue … serving the customer. The company could identify every contact between the customer and the employee, and they could treat that contact as a "moment of truth." Carlson set out to let his people know the importance of that moment for the captain, the ticket agent, the baggage handler, the flight attendant. … "Every moment, every contact," he said, "must be as pleasant and memorable as possible." He figured that he had approximately 10 million customers each year, and on average, each customer had contact with five of his people for approximately 15 seconds apiece. Therefore, in his mind, these 50 million contacts, 15 seconds at a time, would determine the fate of his company.

Jan Carlson had a vision to share with 20,000 employees. He had to empower his "front line," inspire them to make the decisions and take action—because they were Scandinavian Airlines during those 15 seconds. He now had 20,000 people who were energized and ready to go because they were focused on one very important thing …"to make every second count."

I wonder what we could accomplish if we decided to *"make every moment count!"*

WHAT DO YOU THINK?

_____
_____
_____
_____
_____
_____
_____
_____
_____
_____
_____
_____
_____
_____
_____
_____
_____
_____
_____

6 MORE THOUGHTS FOR YOUR WEEK:
TURNAROUNDS

"Obstacles don't have to stop you. If you run into a wall, don't turn around and give up. Figure out how to climb it, go through it, or work around it."

—MICHAEL JORDAN

"It's worth recognizing that there is no such thing as an overnight success. You will do well to cultivate the resources in yourself that bring you happiness outside of success or failure. The truth is, most of us discover where we are headed when we arrive. At that time, we turn around and say, yes, this is obviously where I was going all along. It's a good idea to try to enjoy the scenery on the detours, because you'll probably take a few."

—BILL WATTERSON

"Chains of habit are too light to be felt until they are too heavy to be broken."

—WARREN BUFFETT

"Iron rusts from disuse; water loses its purity from stagnation and in cold weather becomes frozen; so inaction saps the vigors of the mind."

—LEONARDO DA VINCI

"I have always found that if I move with seventy-five percent or more of the facts, that I usually never regret it. It's the guys who wait to have everything perfect that drive you crazy."

—LEE IACOCCA

"A dead end street is a good place to turn around."

—NAOMI JUDD

"Energy and persistence conquer all things."

–BENJAMIN FRANKLIN

STATESMAN, WRITER, INVENTOR

I WAS JUST THINKING ABOUT … PERSISTENCE

Persistence, perseverance, determination, doggedness, resolve … all are the same bedfellows, the "fuel" that helps you get the job done. One of my favorite stories about persistence I heard from my friend Zig Ziglar, author of numerous best-sellers, including *See You at the Top,* which has sold more than 1.6 million copies:

In 1933, Charles Darrow brought "Monopoly" to the Parker Brothers Company. The "experts" at Parker Brothers rejected the game, citing "52 fundamental errors."

Ironically, in 1936, Mr. Darrow was well received by the embarrassed Parker Brothers. See, the persistent Charles Darrow had spent the year of his rejection demonstrating the potential success of the game by selling numerous editions of the board game himself. Parker Brothers eventually helped make the unemployed heating engineer from Germantown, PA, a multi-millionaire. Since that time, over 275 million copies of Monopoly have been sold in 111 countries and 43 languages! Each year, Parker Brothers prints $40 billion worth of Monopoly money—more than twice the amount printed annually by the U.S. Mint! Monopoly's success has produced more than six billion of those little green houses … enough, I'm told, to circle the globe!

Today, with 485 million players around the globe, Monopoly is the most commercially successful board game in the world.

Another classic story about persistence is captured in a most unusual tombstone. The famous battle cry, "Remember the Alamo," was a phrase written by a young man who was a journalist living in Texas in the early 1880s. He also dreamed of finding a way "to make a potato into a pill box, a pumpkin into a tablespoon, and a watermelon into a saucer." In the 1850s, when the California gold rush took place, he invented a dehydrated meat biscuit that had limited success. But the dream that consumed him the most came to him as he returned home from a trip abroad to England. He saw children dying as a result of drinking contaminated milk. He decided to dedicate the rest of his life to finding a way to make milk safe for human consumption.

Through his experiments with the biscuits, he knew food could be kept for a long time if moisture was reduced. He kept trying and trying, and finally, he found a way to evaporate the water in milk. The United States Army placed the first big order—500 pounds—for what he called "condensed milk."

This process became the basis for a multi-billion dollar company, the modern-day dairy business. His name was Gail Borden Jr.. He died in 1874, and on his tombstone it says, "I tried and failed. I tried again and I succeeded."

It's all too easy to procrastinate and not put in the necessary effort for a dream to happen. But try tapping into a "try, try again" persistent attitude. You CAN create a better life!

WHAT DO YOU THINK?

---

6 MORE THOUGHTS FOR YOUR WEEK: PERSISTENCE

"There is no chance, no destiny, no fate that can hinder
or control the firm resolve of a determined soul."

–ELLA WHEELER WILCOX

"It's what you've learned after you know it all that counts."

–JOHN WOODEN

"Making your mark on the world is hard. If it were easy, everybody would do it.
But it's not. It takes patience, it takes commitment, and it comes with plenty of
failure along the way. The real test is not whether you avoid this failure, because
you won't. It's whether you let it harden or shame you into inaction, or whether
you learn from it; whether you choose to persevere."

–BARACK OBAMA

"Perseverance is a great element of success. If you only knock long enough
and loud enough at the gate, you are sure to wake somebody up."

–HENRY WADSWORTH LONGFELLOW

"Patience and perseverance have a magical effect before
which difficulties disappear and obstacles vanish."

–JOHN QUINCY ADAMS

"When you come to the end of your rope, tie a knot and hang on."

–FRANKLIN D. ROOSEVELT

■

"Do as the heavens have done, forget your evil; with them forgive yourself."

—WILLIAM SHAKESPEARE
PLAYWRIGHT

I WAS JUST THINKING ABOUT ... FORGIVENESS

I admire people who make a difference in the world. They have a quality of life that separates them from the rest of the pack. One of these people was the pioneering American nurse and humanitarian Clara Barton.

Clara Barton never harbored resentments. One time a friend recalled to her a cruel thing that had happened to her some years previously, but Clara did not seem to remember it. "Don't you remember the wrong that was done to you?" asked the friend.

"No, I distinctly remember forgetting that," answered Clara.

How can anyone forgive like that? I remember hearing David Augsburger, professor of pastoral care at Fuller Theological Seminary in Pasadena, CA, make a wonderful presentation in which he said:

Forgiveness is a journey of many steps taken carefully, including:

- To see the other as having worth again, regardless of wrongdoing.
- To see the other as equally precious again, in spite of pain felt.
- To cancel demands on the past, recognizing that changing the unchangeable is impossible.
- To work through the anger and pain felt by both in reciprocal trusting and risking until genuineness in intention is perceived and repentance is seen by both to be authentic.
- To drop the demands for an ironclad guarantee of future behavior.

Psalms of My Life

Lord of the compost heap,
you take garbage
and turn it into
soil, good soil,
for seeds to root
and grow
with wildest increase,
flowers to bloom
with brilliant beauty.
Take all the garbage
of my life,
Lord of the compost heap,
turn it into
soil, good soil,
and then plant seeds
to bring forth
fruit and beauty
in profusion.
–Joseph Bayly

Maybe that's why Professor Augsburger and Horace Bushnell both wrote, "Forgiveness is man's deepest need and God's highest achievement."

This helps me understand one of the reasons IBM became such a great company. The story is often told about Thomas Watson Jr., the son of the founder, who also led the company into some of its greatest days. Evidently, a manager of an IBM project that lost $3 million before it was scrapped was called into a meeting with Mr. Watson. "I suppose you want my resignation?" he asked. "Resignation nothing!" replied Mr. Watson. "We've just spent $3 million *educating* you!"

WHAT DO YOU THINK?

6 MORE THOUGHTS FOR YOUR WEEK:
FORGIVENESS

"Doing an injury puts you below your enemy; revenging one
makes you even with him; forgiving it sets you above him."

–Benjamin Franklin

"Forgive your enemies, but never forget their names."

–John F. Kennedy

"To err is human, to forgive divine."

–Alexander Pope

"Wrongs are often forgiven, but contempt never is.
Our pride remembers it forever."

–Lord Chesterfield

"Forgiveness is the fragrance that the violet sheds
on the heel that has crushed it."

–Mark Twain

"When you forgive, you in no way change
the past–but you sure do change the future."

–Bernard Meltzer

■

"The foolish man
seeks happiness
in the distance;
the wise grows
it under his feet."

–JAMES OPPENHEIM
AMERICAN POET, NOVELIST AND EDITOR

I WAS JUST THINKING ABOUT ... HAPPINESS

A friend named Cavett Robert was raised in a small town in Mississippi and went on to become a New York lawyer. In fact, he was the lawyer for a young man named Dale Carnegie, who wanted Cavett to prepare the paper for his company and a program called the "Dale Carnegie Course."

Later, Cavett moved to Phoenix, where he was a wonderful professional speaker and started the National Speakers Association. One night, after dinner, he gave me a copy of a paper he had made for friends called, "Little Known Facts About Well-Known People." The paper only had one story, but I've never forgotten the story, a real classic, or the reason it is so important. Here's what his paper said:

"Sometimes the sources of our happiness contain seeds of our own destruction. Consider General John A. Sutter. On January 24, 1848, one of his workmen who was building a grist mill on the south fork of the American River found a small yellow stone that appeared to be gold. The next morning at daybreak, the man rushed forty miles down the canyon to Sutter's ranch house with the exciting news. Sutter was elated, his heart filled

Dr. Norman Vincent Peale on Happiness

One of my favorite stories on happiness is the response Dr. Peale made in Chicago when asked after a presentation, "Who decides if you are happy or unhappy?" Dr. Peale answered, "You do."

He told about having a conversation over dinner in a railway car with a couple during a business trip. The woman was dressed in expensive furs, diamonds, designer clothing. But rather loudly, she declared the rail car dingy and drafty, the service poor and the food terrible.

Her husband, in contrast, was a pleasant, easy-going, enjoyable man. During dinner, Peale asked the man what business he was in. He said he was a lawyer, and his wife was in manufacturing.

This was surprising, as she did not appear to be the industrial type. So Peale asked, "What does she manufacture?"

"Unhappiness," replied the man. "She manufactures her own unhappiness."

with ultimate happiness. Gold on his land! Pure, yellow nuggets!! He could literally become the richest man on Earth!

"Sutter tried to keep his discovery a secret, but within a day all his ranch hands left their tasks in a mad frenzy, digging and panning and scratching for gold. Within a week, the whole countryside was in turmoil as ranches, towns and villages were abandoned—everyone rushing to Sutter's ranch in search of gold.

"Telegraph wires hummed, and soon soldiers were deserting from the army, fathers from their families, employees from their jobs, farmers from their ranches. ... Half the country appeared to be camping on Sutter's ranch, digging for gold. Ships had no sooner docked in San Francisco Bay before the sailors jumped ship and headed for the hills.

"John Sutter could only look on in helpless rage as his ranch was ransacked, his barns torn down, his crops trampled and his cattle slaughtered. In time, he fought back by filing, what was at that time, the largest lawsuit in history. He claimed that both San Francisco and Sacramento had been built on his property. He won the suit, but never received a penny. Mobs, enraged by the decision, burned down the court-house with its records and blew up Sutter's houses and barns with dynamite. They murdered one of his sons and drove a second to suicide. A third son, in an attempt to escape the madness, fled to Europe, only to drown before reaching land. John A. Sutter, staggering under these cruel blows, lost his reason.

"For 20 years after that, Sutter haunted the Capitol in Washington, trying to persuade Congress to recognize his rights. Dressed in rags, the poor, old, demented gentleman went from one senator to another, pleading for justice. The children in the street laughed at him as he passed.

"In the spring of 1880, Sutter died alone. He didn't have a dollar when he passed away, though he possessed a legal deed to the greatest fortune on Earth."

I wish the General had known Fanny Crosby, one of America's greatest and most prolific hymn writers ... hymns filled with power, promise and purpose. But when Fanny was only six weeks old, she was blinded by a doctor who mistakenly put the wrong solution on her then inflamed eyes. Not defeated, her attitude grew stronger as she grew up, leading her to create a lifetime of uplifting music. One of her first poems expressed remarkable wisdom for a child of only eight:

Oh, what a happy child am I,
Although I cannot see!

I am resolved that in this world,
Contented I will be.

How many blessings I enjoy
That other people don't.
To weep and whine because I'm blind
I cannot—and I won't!

WHAT DO YOU THINK?

_____
_____
_____
_____
_____
_____
_____
_____
_____
_____
_____
_____
_____
_____
_____

6 MORE THOUGHTS FOR YOUR WEEK: HAPPINESS

"If only we'd stop trying to be happy we'd have a pretty good time."
—EDITH WHARTON

"Of all the unhappy people in the world, the unhappiest are those
who have not found something that they want to do."
—JOHN RUSKIN

"There are as many nights as days, and the one is just as long as the
other in the year's course. Even a happy life cannot be without a
measure of darkness, and the word 'happy' would lose its
meaning if it were not balanced by sadness."
—CARL JUNG

"It's so important to know that you can choose to feel good.
Most people don't think they have that choice."
—NEIL SIMON

"Let us be grateful to people who make us happy;
they are the charming gardeners who make our souls blossom."
—MARCEL PROUST

"Happiness is as a butterfly which, when pursued, is always beyond our grasp,
but which, if you will sit down quietly, may alight upon you."
—NATHANIEL HAWTHORNE

■

"Humility is not thinking less of yourself; it's thinking of yourself less."

–RICK WARREN

MINISTER AND AUTHOR

I WAS JUST THINKING ABOUT ... HUMILITY

A famous conductor on a nationwide talk show was asked which instrument he considered the most difficult to play. His reply: "Second fiddle."

British pastor George Duncan wrote: "One of the most important lessons is learning to play second fiddle well. Think for a moment how often we come across those whose worth is seldom recognized by men. Many are prepared to recognize the prominent part played by Simon Peter among the disciples, but forget that if there had not been an Andrew who 'brought him to Jesus' there would never have been a Peter!

"The church gives thanks to God for Paul, the greatest Christian who ever lived, but forgets that if there had not been a Barnabas, there might never have been a Paul! How many recognize the name Albert McMakin? Albert was the young man who invited and took 16-year-old Billy Graham to the evangelistic services where he accepted Christ as his Savior. So before there was a Billy, there had to be an Albert!"

Bloom Where You Are Planted

"Father, where shall I work today?"
And my love flowed warm and free.
Then He pointed me out a tiny spot,
And said, "Tend that for me."
I answered quickly, "Oh no, not that.
Why no one would ever see,
No matter how well my work was done.
Not that little place for me!"
And the word He spoke, it was not stern,
He answered me tenderly,
"Ah little one, search that heart of thine;
Art thou working for them or me?
Nazareth was a little place,
And so was Galilee."
—*Unknown author*

The point is simple—put yourself last and others first.

People always say how much they admire those with humility, but few can tell you what humility really is.

Someone once told me, "Humility is like underwear. We should have it, but not let it show."

I remember hearing Warren Bennis, a wonderful speaker and writer, tell an audience, "Real leaders are people who are notable for their self-possession. They know who they are, have healthy egos and take more pride in what they do than in who they are. They take compliments with a grain of salt and intelligent criticism without rancor. These people learn from their mistakes and don't harp on the mistakes of others. They are gracious winners and losers."

I've always loved this story from presidential history about humility. After Abraham Lincoln defeated Stephen A. Douglas for the presidency, the two were together on the east portico of the Capitol for Lincoln's inauguration. The President-Elect was introduced by Senator Edward E. Baker of Oregon. Lincoln stood beside him, carrying the manuscript of his speech, a cane and his tall silk hat. As he made ready to speak, he looked for a place to put his hat. Stephen Douglas stepped forward, took the hat, and returned to his seat. "If I can't be President," he said to a cousin of Mrs. Lincoln, "I can at least hold his hat."

WHAT DO YOU THINK?

6 MORE THOUGHTS FOR YOUR WEEK: HUMILITY

"Humility makes great men twice honorable."

–BENJAMIN FRANKLIN

"The life of every man is a diary in which he means to write one story,
and writes another, and his humblest hour is when he compares
the volume as it is with what he vowed to make."

–J.M. BARRIE

"If I only had a little humility, I would be perfect."

–TED TURNER

"There are a billion people in China. It's not easy to be an individual in a crowd
of more than a billion people. Think of it. More than a BILLION people.
That means even if you're a one-in-a-million type of guy,
there are still a thousand guys exactly like you."

–A. WHITNEY BROWN

"Man is great only when he is kneeling."

–POPE PIUS XII

"When science discovers the center of the universe,
a lot of people will be disappointed to find they are not it."

–BERNARD BAILY

"Take away
love and
our Earth
is a tomb."

—ROBERT BROWNING
ENGLISH POET AND PLAYWRIGHT

I WAS JUST THINKING ABOUT ... LOVE

You really can't explain love—you just have to feel it.

One evening just before the great Broadway musical star Mary Martin was to go onstage in *South Pacific*, a note was handed to her. It was from Oscar Hammerstein, the show's lyricist, who at that moment was on his deathbed. The note simply said:

"Dear Mary: A bell's not a bell till you ring it. A song's not a song till you sing it. Love in your heart is not put there to stay. Love isn't love till you give it away."

After her performance that night, many people rushed backstage, crying, "Mary, what happened to you out there tonight? We never saw anything like that before." Blinking back tears, Mary read them the note from Hammerstein. Then she said, "Tonight I gave my love away."

Donald Grey Barnhouse, one of America's most treasured speakers and writers, and for years the pastor of the Tenth Presbyterian Church in Philadelphia, was asked to help people understand real love. This is what he wrote:

"Love is the key. Joy is love singing. Peace is love resting. Long-suffering is love enduring. Kindness is love's touch. Goodness is love's character. Faithfulness is love's habit. Gentleness is love's self-forgetfulness. Self-control is love holding the reins."

Then when asked to give an illustration of real love, he told the following story:

A little boy was told by his doctor that he could save his sister's life if he gave her some blood. The six-year-old girl was near death, a victim of a disease that the boy had miraculously recovered from two years earlier. Her only chance was a blood transfusion from someone who had previously conquered the illness. Since the children were both rare blood types, the little boy was an ideal candidate. "Johnny, would you give your blood for Mary?" asked the doctor.

The boy hesitated. His lower lip started to tremble, but then he smiled and said, "Sure, I'll give my blood for my sister."

Soon the two children were wheeled into the operating room—Mary, pale and thin; Johnny, robust and the picture of health. Neither spoke, but when their eyes met, Johnny grinned. As his blood siphoned into Mary's veins, one could almost see new life come into her tired body. The ordeal was nearly over when Johnny's voice broke the silence: "Say, Doc? When do I die?"

Only then did the doctor realize what the moment of hesitation and trembling lip had meant earlier. Johnny thought that in giving his blood to his sister, he would be giving up his life! And in that brief moment, Johnny had made a brave—and *loving*—decision.

WHAT DO YOU THINK?

6 MORE THOUGHTS FOR YOUR WEEK: LOVE

"I have found that if you love life, life will love you back."

–ARTHUR RUBENSTEIN

"Happiness is only in loving."

–LEO TOLSTOY

"Love is life...and if you miss love, you miss life."

–LEO BUSCAGLIA

"The grand essentials to happiness in this life are something to do,
someone to love, and something to hope for."

–JOSEPH ADDISON

"Love does not consist of gazing at each other,
but in looking together in the same direction."

–ANTOINE DE SAINT-EXUPERY

"Love: a temporary insanity, curable by marriage."

–AMBROSE BIERCE

■

"The illiterate of the 21st century will not be those who cannot read and write, but those who cannot learn, unlearn, and relearn."

—ALVIN TOFFLER

WRITER AND EDUCATOR

I WAS JUST THINKING ABOUT ... LEARNING

This art-of-living jewel is from Cicero, the Roman statesman and philosopher. It was written some 2,000 years ago. His wisdom is still a cornerstone for living ... and learning ... today.

The Six Mistakes of Man

- The delusion that personal gain is made by crushing others.
- The tendency to worry about things that cannot be changed or corrected.
- Insisting that a thing is impossible because we cannot accomplish it.
- Refusing to set aside trivial preferences.
- Neglecting development and refinement of the mind, and not acquiring the habit of reading and studying.
- Attempting to compel others to believe and live as we do.

WHAT DO YOU THINK?

6 MORE THOUGHTS FOR YOUR WEEK: LEARNING

"When an old man dies, a library burns down."
–AFRICAN PROVERB

"Every man who rises above the common level has received
two educations: the first from his teachers; the second,
more personal and more important, from himself."
–EDWARD GIBBON

"You don't have to know everything to be happy—in fact, it helps."
–RUSS EDIGER

"There can be as much value in the blink
of an eye as in months of rational analysis."
–MALCOLM GLADWELL

"Whoso neglects learning in his youth,
Loses the past and is dead for the future."
–EURIPIDES

"Man's mind, once stretched by a new idea,
never regains its original dimensions."
–OLIVER WENDELL HOLMES

■

"Talent without discipline is like an octopus on roller skates. There's plenty of movement, but you never know if it's going to be forward, backwards, or sideways."

H. JACKSON BROWN JR.
AUTHOR

SELF-DISCIPLINE

When I reach for a glass of juice, this story about self-discipline often pours forth in my mind. A deeply religious dentist cringed at the thought that wine was being used in his church's communion service. He thought somebody should come up with a non-alcoholic substitute. In 1869, he decided he would give it a try.

He lived in a town called Vineyard, NJ, named such because of the numerous vineyards. It was common for him to see bushels of fruit as payment for his dental services. He started to experiment in his kitchen, trying to create a grape beverage that would not ferment and become alcoholic.

It took decades of self-discipline to stick with his goal, over 20 years in fact. But one day his "unfermented wine" appeared as an option for a family refreshment in his small town. In 1892, his youngest son, Charles, who was also a dentist, decided to test out his long-held belief that the grape drink could be successful as a commercial product. With the idea of making the beverage more appealing to the general public, he changed the name to "Welch's Grape Juice." He introduced the new drink in Chicago, and the rest, as they say, is history.

Dr. Thomas Welch, in his last public appearance, said, "This proves what I've always believed. God doesn't give you dreams to taunt you!" All it took was discipline. And today Welch's is the world's leading producer of more than 400 Concord and Niagara grape-based products—sold in more than 35 countries.

WHAT DO YOU THINK?

6 MORE THOUGHTS FOR YOUR WEEK:
SELF-DISCIPLINE

"Rule your mind or it will rule you."

–HORACE

"If you seek to lead, invest at least 50 percent of your time leading yourself—your own purpose, ethics, principles, motivation, conduct. Invest at least 20 percent leading those with authority over you and 15 percent leading your peers. If you don't understand that you work for your mislabeled 'subordinates,' then you know nothing of leadership. You know only tyranny."

— DEE HOCK, FOUNDER AND CEO EMERITUS, VISA INTERNATIONAL

"I am, indeed, a king, because I know how to rule myself."

–PIETRO ARETINO

"Respect your efforts, respect yourself. Self-respect leads to self-discipline. When you have both firmly under your belt, that's real power."

–CLINT EASTWOOD

"In reading the lives of great men, I found that the first victory they won was over themselves ... self-discipline with all of them came first."

–HARRY S TRUMAN

"Dreams get you started; discipline keeps you going."

–JIM ROHN

■

"Whenever anyone has offended me, I try to raise my soul so high that the offense cannot reach it."

—RENÉ DESCARTES
FRENCH MATHEMATICIAN AND PHILOSOPHER

I WAS JUST THINKING ABOUT ... SELF-ESTEEM

In difficult times, self-esteem can take a real beating. We could all learn a lesson from an amazing man named Charles Steinmetz, who was a pioneering genius in harnessing electricity. His story provides a wonderful perspective on confidence and self-esteem.

First, a word about the challenges facing Steinmetz. He suffered from dwarfism and was a hunchback, just like his father and grandfather, and before completing his doctorate he had to flee German police, ostensibly for supporting socialist causes. But, shortly after arriving in the United States in 1889, he got a job with a company producing transformers, which was purchased by General Electric. Awkwardness, unpleasant encounters, upheavals settling in a new country--all stalked the brilliant young man.

Steinmetz lost himself in his work. He documented the phenomenon of alternating current and created artificial lightning in a football-field-sized lab using 120,000-volt generators. His research was groundbreaking. Even after he retired, his former employees at GE still relied on his brilliance. Such was the case when an intricate set of machines broke down. In-house experts could not find the cause of the malfunction, so Steinmetz was called in to have a look.

After testing various parts, Steinmetz pinpointed the problem and marked the defective part with a chalk mark. He then submitted a bill for $10,000.

Surprised at this unexpectedly high price, GE mangers asked Steinmetz to resubmit an itemized invoice. He compiled a new statement that listed only two items:

Making one chalk mark: $1.00
Knowing where to place it: $9,999.00

6 MORE THOUGHTS FOR YOUR WEEK: SELF-ESTEEM

"God didn't make a mistake when He made you.
You need to see yourself as God sees you."
–JOEL OSTEEN

"The greatest discovery in the last 100 years is the self-image.
It chooses our mate, our friends, our occupation,
and even sets the limits of our ability to perform."
–DR. JOYCE BROTHERS

"Remember, no one can make you feel inferior without your consent."
–ELEANOR ROOSEVELT

"Always be a first-rate version of yourself,
instead of a second-rate version of somebody else."
–JUDY GARLAND

"Do not wish to be anything but what you are,
and try to be that perfectly."
–ST. FRANCIS DE SALES

"Beauty comes in all ages, colors, shapes, and forms.
God never makes junk."
–KATHY IRELAND

■

"From what we get,
we can make
a living;
what we give,
however,
makes a life."

—ARTHUR ASHE
TENNIS CHAMPION

MONEY VERSUS A LIFE

I heard this story from Cavett Robert, founder of the National Speakers Association and considered the "Dean of Public Speaking." It was a favorite of his. He was talking about a meeting back in 1923 at the Edgewater Beach Hotel in Chicago. At that meeting were eight of America's most powerful men:

1. Charles Schwab: President of America's largest independent steel company
2. Samuel Insull: President of America's greatest utility company
3. Howard Hopson: President of America's largest gas company
4. Richard Whitney: President of the New York Stock Exchange
5. Albert Fall: Member of the President's Cabinet
6. Jesse Livermore: Leading Wall Street financier
7. Ivan Kruger: Head of the world's largest monopoly
8. Leon Fraser: President of the Bank of International Settlements

But then Robert pointed out where these same men were 25 years later. ...

1. Charles Schwab: Lived on borrowed money the last five years of his life, dying bankrupt
2. Samuel Insull: Died penniless, as a fugitive from justice
3. Howard Hopson: Dead
4. Richard Whitney: Just earned his release from Sing Sing Correctional Facility
5. Albert Fall: Pardoned from prison to die at home
6. Jesse Livermore: Committed suicide
7. Ivan Kruger: Committed suicide
8. Leon Fraser: Also committed suicide

The point is, they made all that money, but they couldn't make a life!

WHAT DO YOU THINK?

6 MORE THOUGHTS FOR YOUR WEEK:
MONEY VERSUS A LIFE

"If money is your hope for independence, you will never have it. The only real security that a man will have in this world is a reserve of knowledge, experience, and ability."

–HENRY FORD

"Money is better than poverty, if only for financial reasons."

–WOODY ALLEN

"Everything you want in life has a price connected to it. There's a price to pay if you want to make things better, a price to pay just for leaving things as they are, a price for everything."

–HARRY BROWNE

"Focusing your life solely on making a buck shows a certain poverty of ambition. It asks too little of yourself. Because it's only when you hitch your wagon to something larger than yourself that you realize your true potential."

–BARACK OBAMA

"I absolutely believe in the power of tithing and giving back. My own experience about all the blessings I've had in my life is that the more I give away, the more that comes back. That is the way life works, and that is the way energy works."

–KEN BLANCHARD

"We make a living by what we get, but we make a life by what we give."

–WINSTON CHURCHILL

■

"It is a good thing to have all the props pulled out from under us occasionally. It gives us some sense of what is rock under our feet and what is sand."

MADELEINE L'ENGLE

I WAS JUST THINKING ABOUT ...
FACING TROUBLE HEAD-ON

Growing up I loved to be around and looked up to West Texas cowboys. I remember them telling me about a lesson to be learned from cattle.

In the terrible winter blizzards, most cattle would turn their backs to the icy wind and slowly drift downwind until they reached a boundary fence. With nowhere further to go, the cattle would stand motionless and helpless against the wind and snow. They would slowly become covered with ice and snow, dying by the scores.

But Hereford cattle responded differently.

These cattle would instinctively head toward the windy blasts, stand shoulder to shoulder with bowed heads to face nature's onslaught. You almost always found Hereford cattle alive and well once the storm passed.

The cowboys told me that was the greatest lesson you could learn on the prairie: just to meet adversity head-on and face life's storms.

New Meaning for "Trouble"

"In the Chinese language, entire words and concepts are written with one symbol. Sometimes these symbols are combined to make a new meaning or word. The two individual Chinese characters used separately to mean trouble and crisis both carry negative connotations. However, when brought together and used as a pair, the two mean something entirely opposite: opportunity."
–It's Always Too Soon to Quit

I read a story recently about a 67-year-old man who stood on a curb and watched his life's work burn up in December 1914. Adding insult to injury, his property was only insured for $238,000. ... far less than the $2,000,000 worth of damage. His 24-year-old son, Charles, said, "My heart aches for him. He was 67, no longer a young man, and everything was going up in flames." When Charles found his father that night, however, he was surprised to hear his dad's request. He said, "Find your mother and bring her here. She will never again see anything like this as long as she lives." The next morning, the old man gathered his employees at the charred ruins and said, "There is great value in disaster. All of our mistakes are burned up—thank God we can start anew!"

Three weeks later, Thomas Edison delivered to us his first phonograph.

How do you explain this ability? I'm not sure, but maybe it was best explained by Dr. Norman Vincent Peale when he said, "Great people rise above adversity by turning tribulations into triumphs, failures into fortunes and burdens into blessings!"

WHAT DO YOU THINK?

6 MORE THOUGHTS FOR YOUR WEEK:
FACING TROUBLE

"If it turns out that my best wasn't good enough, at least I won't look back and say that I was afraid to try; failure makes me work even harder."

–MICHAEL JORDAN

"It is by going down into the abyss that we recover the treasures of life. Where you stumble, there lies your treasure."

–JOSEPH CAMPBELL

"The harder the conflict, the more glorious the triumph. What we obtain too cheap, we esteem too lightly; 'tis dearness only that gives everything its value."

–THOMAS PAINE

"Out of difficulties grow miracles."

–JEAN DE LA BRUYERE

"It is defeat that turns bone into flint, and gristle to muscle and makes people invincible, and formed those heroic natures that are now in ascendancy in the world. Do not, then, be afraid of defeat. You are never so near to victory as when defeated in a good cause."

–HENRY WARD BEECHER

"It's in the struggle itself that you define yourself."

–PAT BUCHANAN

■

"Sometimes our fate resembles a fruit tree in winter. Who would think that those branches would turn green again and blossom, but we hope, we know it."

– JOHANN WOLFGANG VON GOETHE
GERMAN WRITER

I WAS JUST THINKING ABOUT … SELF-RELIANCE

My grandfather used to tell this story to teach all of us grandkids self-reliance. "Believe in yourself and follow your dreams," he said, "instead of allowing others to determine what you can be." Funny thing is, I like to tell it to myself today. So here's his story that has passed the test of time:

A young Native American found a lone eagle egg that had been abandoned. To be helpful, the Native American placed it in a nest of a prairie chicken.

The little eagle grew up with the prairie chicks—clucking and pecking around on the ground as they dug for insects, worms and seeds. When he flew, he never got more than a few feet off the ground—same as the rest of the birds. Life was one pleasant day after another, and soon enough, the eagle grew and matured.

One day, as he was pecking the ground for food, something caught the eagle's eye. He glanced upward, and there, soaring in the clouds, was the most splendid bird he had ever seen. He couldn't take his eyes off the bird's gorgeous, strong, golden wings that never seemed to move as the unusual creature commanded the sky.

Fix-It-Yourself 101

"A man sooner or later discovers that he is the master-gardener of his soul, the director of his life."
–James Allen

The eagle raced over to the head prairie chicken and asked, "What is that stunning, noble bird flying over the treetops?"

The senior prairie chick looked up and replied, "Oh, that is the Eagle, Chief of Birds. But he is far above you. Keep scratching."

So, following the advice of others, the eagle went back to scratching the ground and never realized he was more than just a prairie chicken.

WHAT DO YOU THINK?

6 MORE THOUGHTS FOR YOUR WEEK:
SELF-RELIANCE

"The best place to find a helping hand is at the end of your own arm."
—SWEDISH PROVERB

"God loves to help him who strives to help himself."
—AESCHYLUS

"Real adulthood is the result of two qualities: self-discipline and self-reliance.
The process of developing them together in balance is called maturing."
—J.W. JEPSON

"I don't want to be a passenger in my own life."
—DIANE ACKERMAN

"The best lightning rod for your protection is your own spine."
—RALPH WALDO EMERSON

"Pray hard, work hard, and leave the rest to God."
—FLORENCE GRIFFITH JOYNER

■

"No single raindrop
ever considers itself
responsible
for the flood."

—JOHN RUSKIN
BRITISH SOCIAL THINKER

I WAS JUST THINKING ABOUT …

RESPONSIBILITY

The good news is that each person is uniquely gifted to do something different, and that some of those gifts in life are done in quiet ways that the world may never see or know. This story always inspires me:

In Maine they tell of an old man walking along the beach with his grandson. The boy picked up each starfish they passed and threw it back into the sea. "If I left them here," the boy said, "they would dry up and die. I'm saving their lives."

Said the old man, "But the beach goes on for miles, and there are millions of starfish. What you are doing won't make any difference."

The boy looked at the starfish in his hand, gently threw it back into the ocean and answered, "It makes a difference to this one."

As John W. Newbern said, "People can be divided into three groups: those who make things happen, those who watch things happen and those who wonder what happened." Isn't it time to take responsibility for all corners of your life and make things happen?

A Better You

"'Your task is to behold a better world,'
said God.
And I answered, 'How?'
'The world is such a large, vast place
And so complicated now.'

'And I'm so small and useless.
There is nothing I can do.'
But God—in all His wisdom said,
'You just build a better you!'"
—*Author Unknown*

WHAT DO YOU THINK?

_____

_____

_____

6 MORE THOUGHTS FOR YOUR WEEK:
RESPONSIBILITY

"If you want children to keep their feet on the ground,
put some responsibility on their shoulders."

–Abigail Van Buren

"In passing, also, I would like to say that the first time
Adam had a chance he laid the blame on a woman."

–Nancy Astor

"The smallest good deed is greater than the grandest good intention."

–Japanese Proverb

An African parable says, "*Every morning in Africa, a gazelle wakes up. It knows that it
must run faster than the fastest lion or it will be killed. Every morning a lion wakes up.
It knows that it must outrun the slowest gazelle or it will starve to death.*"
It does not matter whether you are a lion or a gazelle:
When the sun comes up, you better be running.

–African Parable

"The man who complains about the way the
ball bounces is likely to be the one who dropped it."

–Lou Holtz

"Always do right.
This will gratify
some and astonish
the rest."

—MARK TWAIN
AUTHOR AND HUMORIST

I WAS JUST THINKING ABOUT …
RIGHT AND WRONG

American showman P.T. Barnum (1810 - 1891), known erroneously for the phrase, "There's a sucker born every minute," may be gone more than 100 years now, but there is something so honorable, so fascinating in his life story that I often refer to him.

Barnum was the founder of one of America's most popular early circuses, which was billed as "the Greatest Show on Earth" and became the Ringling Bros. and Barnum & Bailey Circus. He succeeded in spite of many failures, setbacks and hardships throughout his life. For instance, Barnum left school at eight years of age to help in his father's store. When his father died just a few years later, he took over the store and opened a number of other successful businesses. By age 20, Barnum was quite successful in all of his enterprises. But, at 50, Barnum arranged a business deal with a man who turned out to be a swindler, leaving Barnum $500,000 in debt—and that was in the 1850s! Humiliated, he spent ten years laboring, in part on a lecture tour, to pay back his creditors when all of his remaining business enterprises then failed. He felt obliged to do the right thing. Rather than give up, Barnum decided to open a new business venture, a "Museum of Oddities." When that museum burned down, leaving him once again in massive debt, he opened a traveling circus show.

Although it is not well known and he claims not to have liked politics, Barnum was elected to the Connecticut legislature for two terms and then went on to become mayor of Bridgeport. He founded the Bridgeport Hospital. But his crowning moment actually came in the Connecticut legislature when he took a stand in favor of the Constitutional amendment to abolish slavery, saying, "A human soul is not to be trifled with. It may inhabit the body of a Chinaman, a Turk, an Arab or a Hotentot—it is still an immortal spirit!"

Barnum was certainly one of the greatest showmen of all time, a gifted entrepreneur AND an outstanding public servant. Rumor is that he carried in his pocket a poem given to him by his father:

> Looking back, it seems to me
> All the grief, which had to be,
> Left me when the pain was o'er
> Richer than I'd been before.

I think P.T. Barnum knew something about life, and about what's right and wrong, that would benefit us all!

WHAT DO YOU THINK?

_____

_____

_____

_____

_____

_____

_____

_____

_____

_____

_____

_____

_____

6 MORE THOUGHTS FOR YOUR WEEK:
RIGHT AND WRONG

"I hope they're still making women like my momma. She always told me to do the right thing. She always told me to have pride in myself; she said a good name is better than money."

–Joe Louis

"Let us have faith that right makes right, and in that faith let us to the end dare to do our duty as we understand it."

–Abraham Lincoln

"A quiet conscience sleeps in thunder."

–English proverb

"To be one's self, and unafraid whether right or wrong, is more admirable than the easy cowardice of surrender to conformity."

–Irving Wallace

"Everything happens for a reason. People change so that you can learn to let go. Things go wrong so that you appreciate them when they're right and sometimes good things fall apart so better things can fall together."

–Dr. Laura Schlessinger

"Our greatest happiness does not depend on the condition of life in which chance has placed us, but is always the result of a good conscience, good health, occupation, and freedom in all just pursuits."

–Thomas Jefferson

■

"Other things may change us, but we start and end with family."

—ANTHONY BRANDT
AUTHOR

I WAS JUST THINKING ABOUT … FAMILY

Today would have been my youngest son's birthday. He died nine years ago, and yet not a day goes by I don't think of him, talk to him, miss him terribly. He began going blind when he was 10 years old and was completely blind by age 18. But he never used that as an excuse for doing less than his best. His outlook on life was, "I can't control what happens to me, but I can control how I react to what life does!" Craig not only finished high school, but he finished college too—with a 3.7 out of a 4.0 grade point average.

Someone sent me the following story. I certainly hope it is not true, but I know, as I think about family, it has made an impact on my life:

It was Grandfather's birthday. He was 79. He got up early, shaved, showered, combed his hair and put on his Sunday best so he would look nice when they came.

He skipped his daily walk to the town café where he had coffee with his cronies. He wanted to be sure to be home when they came. He put his porch chair on the sidewalk so he could get a better view of the street when they drove up to help celebrate his birthday. At noon he got tired, but he decided to forgo his nap so he could be there when they came. Most of the rest of the afternoon he spent near the telephone so he could answer it when they called.

He has five children, 13 grandchildren and three great-grandchildren. One son and daughter live within ten miles of the place. They hadn't visited him for a long time. But today was his birthday, and they were sure to come.

At suppertime, he left the cake untouched so they could cut it and have dessert with him.

After supper, he sat on the porch waiting.

At 8:30 he went to his room to prepare for bed. Before retiring, he left a note on the door that said, "Be sure to wake me up when they come."

It was Grandfather's birthday. He was 79.

Your family should be celebrated ... every day. Be sure to do something today so everyone feels appreciated—and can thrive.

WHAT DO YOU THINK?

6 MORE THOUGHTS FOR YOUR WEEK: FAMILY

"Having a child is surely the most beautifully irrational act
that two people in love can commit."

–BILL COSBY

"A happy family is but an earlier heaven."

–ANONYMOUS

"A baby is God's opinion that life should go on."

–CARL SANDBURG

"A family is a unit composed not only of children but of men,
women, an occasional animal, and the common cold."

–OGDEN NASH

"A mother's love waits up when the rest of the
world has already turned out the lights."

–DIANA MANNING

"Families are like fudge ... mostly sweet with a few nuts."

–AUTHOR UNKNOWN

■

"Many people will walk in and out of your life, but only true friends will leave footprints in your heart."

—ELEANOR ROOSEVELT
FIRST LADY AND POLITICAL ACTIVIST

I WAS JUST THINKING ABOUT ... FRIENDS

Andy Rooney of *60 Minutes* fame once said, "Good old friends are worth keeping, whether you like them or not."

That reminds me of a story we tell in Texas about a man named Sam Rayburn. Mr. Sam Rayburn was the Speaker of the United States House of Representatives for 17 years, longer than any other man in our history. The teenage daughter of a friend died suddenly one night. Early the next morning, the father heard a knock on his door—it was Mr. Rayburn.

He said, "I just came by to see what I can do to help." The father replied in his deep grief, "I don't think there is anything you can do. We are making all the arrangements."

"Well," Mr. Rayburn said, "Have you had your coffee this morning?"

The man replied that they had not taken time for breakfast. So Mr. Rayburn said the least he could do was make coffee for them. While he was working in the kitchen, the father said, "I thought you were supposed to be having breakfast at the White House this morning." Mr. Rayburn replied, "Well, I was, but I called the President and told him I had a friend who was in trouble—so I couldn't come."

Think about the joy of friendship ... real, true friendship. This is the kind of friendship described by Eugene Kennedy when he wrote, "The main business of friendship is to sustain and make bearable each other's burdens."

One of my heroes is a Vietnam veteran, a military man who knew the horrors of war, and the value of a friend. I never tire of his telling about an ambush his platoon suffered. He asked his platoon leader if he might go out and bring in one of his comrades who lay grievously wounded. "You can go," said the officer, "but it's not worth it. Your friend is probably killed, and you will throw your own life away."

But the man went. Somehow, despite being injured, he managed to get his friend, hoist him onto his shoulder and bring him back. The officer looked calmly at the would-be rescuer, and then he said, "I told you it wouldn't be worth it. Your friend is dead, and now you are wounded as well."

"It was worth it, though, sir," he said. "Because when I got to him he was still alive, and he said to me, 'I knew you'd come.'"

This story well illustrates the saying, "A friend walks in when the world walks out." And as Andy Rooney noted, good old friends are worth keeping!

WHAT DO YOU THINK?

6 MORE THOUGHTS FOR YOUR WEEK: FRIENDS

"A single rose can be my garden ... a single friend, my world."

–LEO BUSCAGLIA

"True friends visit us in prosperity only when invited,
but in adversity they come without invitation."

–THEOPHRASTUS

"In everyone's life, at some time, our inner fire goes out. It is then burst into
flame by an encounter with another human being. We should all be
thankful for those people who rekindle the inner spirit."

–ALBERT SCHWEITZER

"I don't need a friend who changes when I change and who nods when I nod;
my shadow does that much better."

–PLUTARCH

"Friendship is one of the sweetest joys of life. Many might have failed beneath
the bitterness of their trial, had they not found a friend."

–CHARLES SPURGEON

"Friendship makes prosperity more brilliant,
and lightens adversity by dividing and sharing it."

–CICERO

■

"Pay attention
to your dreams.
God's angels often
speak directly to
our hearts when
we are asleep."

—EILEEN ELIAS FREEMAN
AUTHOR

I WAS JUST THINKING ABOUT ... ANGELS

The last time I spoke on the program with Paul Harvey, the person called "the most listened to man" in broadcasting, who spent seven decades on air and was known for his folksy radio program, "The Rest of the Story," he told a story that made me laugh ... and think ... and laugh.

His story was about a traveler who, between flights at an airport, bought herself a small package of cookies. She then sat down in the busy snack shop to read the newspaper. As she read her paper, she became aware of a rustling noise. Peeking around the newsprint, she was shocked to see a well-dressed gentleman sitting across from her helping himself to her cookies! Half-angry and half-embarrassed, she reached over and gently slid the package closer to herself, and she took one out and began to munch on it.

A minute or so passed before she heard more rustling. The man had gotten another cookie! By now there was only one left in the package. She was flabbergasted; but she didn't want to make a scene, so she said nothing. Finally, as if to add insult to injury, the man broke the remaining cookie in half, pushed one piece across the table toward her with a frown, gulped down his half and left without even saying "thank you." She sat there dumbfounded.

Sometime later, when her flight was announced, the woman opened her bag to get her ticket. To her shock, she discovered in her purse the package of unopened cookies. Somewhere in that same airport, another traveler tried to figure out how that strange woman could have been so insensitive.

I told Paul, "No, no, no! The point is that the woman realized sometimes we meet angels and never even know it!"

WHAT DO YOU THINK?

6 MORE THOUGHTS FOR YOUR WEEK: ANGELS

"A man does not have to be an angel in order to be a saint."
—ALBERT SCHWEITZER

"The golden moments in the stream of life rush past us
and we see nothing but sand; the angels come to visit us,
and we only know them when they are gone."
—GEORGE ELIOT

"Angels can fly because they take themselves lightly."
—G.K. CHESTERTON

"Millions of spiritual creatures walk the earth unseen,
both when we wake and when we sleep."
—JOHN MILTON

"I saw the angel in the marble and carved until I set him free."
—MICHELANGELO

"Do not forget to entertain strangers,
for by so doing some have unwittingly entertained angels."
—HEBREWS 13:2

"To speak gratitude is courteous and pleasant; to enact gratitude is generous and noble, but to live gratitude is to touch Heaven."

—JOHANNES A. GAERTNER
AUTHOR

I WAS JUST THINKING ABOUT ...
LIVING YOUR BEST LIFE

So many people tell me what they could have done—or been—if they had just "gotten a break." I wish I had told them what I know now. We all need to "live gratitude," no matter the circumstances, seizing the opportunities and breaks that DO happen all around us, every day. This is the key to living our best life, the one that touches heaven.

She was quite a lady, but she had a tough time getting to be "quite a lady." Her first job was a copy girl at a small town newspaper. It inspired in her a dream of being a writer for a paper, but when she was in college, she was told, "Forget about being a writer."

When she graduated with a degree in English she did get a job as a writer ... for the obituary column. That year, she began to experience even more adversity. She had married and along with her husband, dreamed of having children. But the doctors said she would never have a family. So they adopted a daughter. Within a year, she was surprised to find herself pregnant. Even that was difficult because in four years, she was pregnant four times, but only two babies survived.

God, Why Don't You Save Me?

Remember the story of the man who was drowning in the ocean? I refer frequently to this story.

A boat approached and offered help. The captain said, "Here, grab on to this life preserver." "No," said the man. "I'm waiting for God to save me." Minutes later a helicopter appeared overhead. The pilot shouted down to the drowning man, "Grab on to this rope!" Again the man said, "No, I'm waiting for God to save me." Shortly after, a submarine surfaced and the hatch opened. "Swim over and we'll pull you in." Once again the man replied, "No, I'm waiting for God to save me."

Finally, with no help in sight, the man called out to the heavens, "God, why don't you save me?" A voice replied from out of the clouds, "I sent you a boat, a helicopter and a submarine. There's not much more I can do!"

213

After 20 years, she convinced her editor to allow her to write a weekly humor column for three dollars an article. After a year, she was offered the chance to write three times a week, and the paper began to syndicate her columns. Soon more than 900 newspapers carried her writing.

For 30 years she wrote a column read by 30 million people in the U.S. and Canada. She published more than 15 books, and she was recognized as one of America's most influential women. She was featured on the cover of *Time*. She actually won over 15 honorary degrees.

But adversity wasn't far away. During that same period of time, she had incredible trials, facing breast cancer and kidney failure. She wrote a sitcom that did not last more than a few episodes on television. She wrote a Broadway play that never made it to opening night. As she battled through the last years of her life, going to daily dialysis treatments, before she died at age 69, she wrote, "I'm not a failure. I failed at doing something. It's a big difference."

I think we can learn and benefit from Erma Bombeck. She always tried to live her best life.

WHAT DO YOU THINK?

6 MORE THOUGHTS FOR YOUR WEEK:
LIVING YOUR BEST LIFE

"Give the world the best you have and the best will come back to you."
—MADELINE BRIDGES

"When I was a young infantry officer at Fort Benning, a lot of old captains had served in World War II and Korea. Boy, did they know about soldiering. I heard this piece of barracks wisdom from these wonderful reserve captains: There was a brand-new second lieutenant who was very ambitious and wanted to be a general. So one night at the officer's club the young officer spotted this old general sitting at the bar. So he went up and said, 'How do I become a general?' And the old general answered, 'Son, you've got to work like a dog. You've got to have moral and physical courage. There may be days you're tired, but you must never show fatigue. You'll be afraid, but you can never show fear. You must always be the leader.' The young officer was so excited by this advice. 'Thank you, sir,' he said, 'so is this how I become a general?' 'No,' said the general, 'that's how you become a first lieutenant, and then you keep doing it over and over and over.' Throughout my career, *I've always tried to do my best today*, think about tomorrow, and maybe dream a bit about the future. But doing your best in the present has to be the rule. You won't become a general unless you become a good first lieutenant."

–COLIN POWELL

"It is a mistake to look too far ahead. Only one
link of the chain of destiny can be handled at a time."

–WINSTON CHURCHILL

"To dare is to lose one's footing momentarily.
To not dare is to lose oneself."
–SOREN KIERKEGAARD

"The goal of life is to make your heartbeat match the beat of the universe,
to match your nature with Nature."
–JOSEPH CAMPBELL

"A man can't make a place for himself in the sun
if he keeps taking refuge under the family tree."
–HELEN KELLER

■

"Go confidently
in the direction
of your dreams.
Live the life you
have imagined."

–HENRY DAVID THOREAU
NATURALIST AND AUTHOR

I WAS JUST THINKING ABOUT... DREAMS

Most folks laughed at this man when he was a kid and called him a "dreamer." It seemed he was always dreaming about ways to make money and doing something to make a difference. When he was 52 years old, after 17 years of selling paper cups, he got a job selling a multi-mixer (an invention that made milkshakes). He managed to sell a big order to a pair of brothers in San Bernardino, CA, who had a hamburger stand. It was going to be a great buy for them because they could make multiple milkshakes at one time—and that's where he saw the potential.

He decided to recommend to the brothers that they open up a series of drive-ins, just like the one they ran in California. He got the right to franchise from the brothers, using their name and the "golden arches" as their symbol, and even the multi-mixers he had sold them.

The man's name was Ray Kroc, and of course, the hamburger stand was McDonald's. He actually changed the lifestyle of this nation ... a kid who kept dreaming of doing something, and of being someone.

Kroc's philosophy of life? "It's always too soon to quit." Today McDonald's is in 117 countries, is listed in *Fortune* magazine as No. 14 in "The World's Most Admired Companies" and is one of the few companies whose stock at the end of June 2009, with all the hammering by the recession, was actually the same as it was a year earlier.

No Pipe Dreams!
One of my favorite sayings on the importance of dreams comes from Oscar Hammerstein, whose musical collaborations include *The King and I*, *South Pacific*, *Oklahoma* and *The Sound of Music*, and who authored an estimated 850 songs:
"If you don't have a dream, how are you going to make a dream come true?"

Another favorite ... a call to boundless dreaming, delivered at a college commencement address that was some years back by Congressman Walter Fauntroy. He stood in front of the graduating students at Harvard University and used a call to greatness when he said:

"The past is yours, learn from it. The present is yours, fulfill it. The future is yours, preserve it. Knowledge is yours, use it. Cancer is yours, cure it. Racism is yours, end it. Injustice is yours, correct it. Sickness is yours, heal it. Ignorance is yours, banish it. War is yours, save it. The world is yours, serve it. The environment is yours, cleanse it. Truth is yours, know it. Don't let anything paralyze your mind, tie your hands, or defeat your spirit. Take the world—not to dominate, but to deliver; not to exploit, but to enrich. Take the dream and inherit the earth."

You are now ready to take your dream, your own personalized dream, and inherit the earth.

WHAT DO YOU THINK?

6 MORE THOUGHTS FOR YOUR WEEK: DREAMS

"If you can imagine it, you can possess it. If you can dream it,
you can become it. If you can envision it, you can attain it.
If you can picture it, you can achieve it."
–WILLIAM ARTHUR WARD

"Dreams are whispers from the soul."
–MARCIA WIEDER

"All men dream, but not equally. Those who dream by night in the dusty
recesses of their minds, wake in the day to find that it was vanity:
but the dreamers of the day are dangerous men, for they may act
on their dreams with open eyes, to make them possible."
–THOMAS E. LAWRENCE

"It takes a lot of courage to show your dreams to someone else."
–ERMA BOMBECK

"Dream no small dreams for they have no power to move the hearts of men."
–JOHANN WOLFGANG VON GOETHE

"Reach high, for stars lie hidden in your soul.
Dream deep, for every dream precedes the goal."
–UNKNOWN

■

ABOUT THE AUTHORS

LEWIS TIMBERLAKE

Called "America's Apostle of Optimism," Lewis Timberlake has served in leadership roles in many civic, religious and political organizations:

Timberlake: A Specialist in Success
- State Campaign Manager for two men who became Governor of Texas
- Vice President, Texas Baptist Men
- President, Texas Law Enforcement and Youth Development Foundation
- President, Texas Historical Association
- Citizen Member, Texas Bank Depository Board
- Chairman, Texas State Commission for the Blind
- President, Texas Jaycees
- Vice President, U.S. Jaycees

Among his many honors:
- Outstanding Young Men of the United States
- The Texas Society for the Prevention of Blindness' *Man of Vision*
- Who's Who in the South and Southwest
- One of the Five Outstanding Young Texans
- The National Jaycees "Hall of Leadership"
- International Who's Who of Intellectuals
- Leading Men in America
- The Institute for Management Studies – Distinguished Faculty Award